BACKYARD
BIRDS

BACKYARD
BIRDS

AN ENTHUSIAST'S GUIDE
TO FEEDING, HOUSING, AND
FOSTERING WILD BIRDS

DR. JANANN V. JENNER

Friedman Group

THINK LIKE A BIRD

You've got to think like a bird to plan a successful bird-feeding area. Most people don't realize that although the kind of food in the feeder is important, the design and placement of your bird feeders will drastically alter the feathered clientele who frequent your yard. Although we tend to think of birds as free-flying spirits, birds are actually quite rigid in their feeding habits. Backyard birds ordinarily include seed, fruit, and insect eaters as well as nectar sippers, but only a handful of species are omnivorous. Common crows, jackdaws, pied currawongs, blue jays, and grackles are exceptional in the wide spectrum of foods they eat, but an Anna's hummingbird will starve to death surrounded by sunflower seed. A brambling scorns all food except insects, while hawfinches prefer large, tough seeds. Birds also specialize in feeding in different strata of vegetation, and this affects their behavior at bird feeders. For example, doves are ground feeders who never cling to hanging feeders; woodpeckers (except the northern flicker) seldom feed on the ground, preferring suspended vertical or horizontal suet feeders; many birds prefer to hunt for insects in the highest treetops and are never drawn to seed feeders; while the vast majority of seed eaters prefer their table to be set about five feet off the ground.

DECISIONS, DECISIONS

Because few homes are designed with bird feeding in mind, the initial planning of your feeder area may present problems. Most houses look inward; they are made to be seen rather than for seeing. You may find that your home doesn't have a perfect place for bird feeding and bird viewing, and like most people, you'll be forced to improvise. As you visualize your bird-feeding area, keep in mind that it must combine these features.

1. It should be visible from your favorite chair (or a comfortable substitute), because once the birds start arriving, you will want to sit and watch them.
2. It should be sufficiently private as birds have terrible table manners and you don't want their mess to detract from the appearance of your property.
3. It should be protected from cold winds.
4. It should offer cover where birds can escape from predators, but it should not be so close to bushes that it becomes a cat-feeding area.

This mountain chickadee is feeding from a mugful of homemade bird treat. The coated wire provides a secure perch, and the small size of this feeder may spark ideas of how to devise a winter feeder that will bring birds right to your window.

© Kent & Donna Dannen

Your Area

BACKYARD
BIRDS

BACKYARD
BIRDS

AN ENTHUSIAST'S GUIDE TO FEEDING, HOUSING, AND FOSTERING WILD BIRDS

DR. JANANN V. JENNER

Friedman Group

A FRIEDMAN GROUP BOOK

ISBN 1-56799-058-4

BACKYARD BIRDS
An Enthusiast's Guide to Feeding, Housing, and Fostering Wild Birds
was prepared and produced by
Michael Friedman Publishing Group, Inc.
15 West 26th Street
New York, New York 10010

Editor: Kelly Matthews
Art Director: Jeff Batzli
Designer: Patrick McCarthy
Photography Researcher: Emilya Naymark

Typeset by Classic Type, Inc.
Color separations by Sele & Color srl.
Printed and bound in China by Leefung–Asco Printers Ltd.

Title page and chapter openers: © Carl R. Sams, II/ Dembinsky Photo Associates
Contents page photograph: Medium Thistle Tube by Aspects; Photography by Jim Messina

DEDICATION

For my bird guru, Lanette S. K. McAndrews,
the Bird Woman of Mount Prospect,
who has forgotten more about backyard-bird feeding
than I will ever know.

TABLE OF CONTENTS

Introduction

"A book about feeding birds in your backyard should only have three chapters," my friend Glenn declared while we were floating in the local swimming hole. "Chapter One: Buy some birdseed. Chapter Two: Toss it on the ground. Chapter Three: Birds will eat it. The end."

If it were only that simple!

SO MANY CHOICES

Your first visit to the bird-feeding department of any well-stocked garden or birding store will demonstrate that bird feeding is much more complicated than Glenn's laid-back plan indicates. First of all, birdseed is a highly variable commodity. As you survey the different sorts of seeds and seed mixes that are available, you'll wonder what's best for the birds. Must you get

pure Niger thistle seed or will the bargain bag of mixed seed do just as well for less than half the price?

To make matters worse, bird feeders come in a bewildering array of sizes, designs, and prices. There are feeders shaped like space stations, troll houses, mandarin hats, ceramic mushrooms, and a range of architectural fantasies from barns and outhouses to lighthouses and miniature mansions complete with gingerbread trim. Even the variety of bird feeders that look like bird feeders can be confusing: the standard platform, hopper, and tube-with-perches designs. All this and I haven't even mentioned the slightly more exotic specialty feeders for dispensing nectar, fruit, and suet. It can be confusing. What should you buy?

NOT JUST FOR ECCENTRIC RETIREES ANYMORE

A quick scan of ads in outdoor and nature magazines will show that manufacturers recognize the potential bonanza in the bird-feeding market. Bird products abound. The incredible variety of products offered to backyard-bird enthusiasts is evidence that this hobby, once the province of retirees with lots of time to cram pinecones with peanut butter, has become big business. Once you become hooked on bird feeding you will have joined the 82.5 million people in North America who participate in this extremely popular interest. Incredibly, nearly one-half of the population in North America that is sixteen years or older feeds wild birds. And millions more can be found in Great Britain and Australia, not to mention throughout the rest of the world.

MULTIPLE REWARDS OF BIRD FEEDING

The thrill of acquiring the perfect bird feeder or birdbath aside, actually feeding the birds is a highly satisfying pastime that can be as casual or as engrossing as you choose. Feeding brings the beauty of birds

© Richard Day

The ideal feeder should be sturdy, easy to fill, and able to hold several pounds of seed so you won't need to fill it every day. It should also allow desirable birds to feed without the intrusion of neighborhood squirrels.

Nothing increases the popularity of your bird-feeding area like a reliable supply of clean drinking and bathing water. Birdbaths can be treacherous for some small birds, so make sure yours is safe and shallow as well as inviting.

within easy range of binoculars (or even the naked eye if you feed them right on your windowsill) and allows a glimpse of wildlife that is otherwise unobtainable. The comings and goings at the feeder, the squabbles over birdseed, the arrival of fledglings, and the overnight appearance of exotic migrants all add a natural drama and extra dimension to our lives. It's also a wonderful way to enjoy nature even if you're not the rugged out-doorsy type. And bird feeding is a relatively inexpensive hobby, especially when compared with passions for collecting antique autos or carved Persian gemstones.

BIRD FOSTERING: MORE THAN JUST A HOBBY

Apart from these pleasures, what I call *bird fostering* (an umbrella term that refers to the general enrichment of local habitat for birds and includes bird feeding, bird gardening, and maintaining birdhouses) allows us to give something back to the environment as we bolster the well-being of the intensely alive, feathered nations who share our backyards and gardens. In one sense, we owe it to them. Not only do birds have to contend with well-fed but still-prowling house cats, but cities, suburbs, and urban sprawl also crowd the land that once belonged

to the ancestors of our birds. Breeding habitats are fragmented and ancient migration routes have become tests of endurance across territory that is increasingly hostile to birds. Wetlands are being drained at an alarming rate, tropical rain forests are being turned into pulpwood and picture frames, and rivers and lakes are choked with pollutants. Birds are only so elastic in their adaptive abilities; when deprived of breeding habitat, they inevitably decline. It is little wonder that as we learn more about bird numbers, many species show downward trends.

THE IMPORTANCE OF BIRD FOSTERING IN NORTH AMERICA

In North America, the situation is bleak. A study released by the United States National Academy of Sciences in June 1990 shows declines in many of North America's songbirds. Of the fifty-six species of birds surveyed from 1978 to 1987, 70 percent suffered declines. Many populations are dropping at a rate of 1 to 2 percent each year, and if this loss continues, songbirds will soon become rare on the continent of North America.

There are multiple causes for the declines in North American bird populations: real estate development gobbles up and fragments breeding habitat and deforestation in faraway tropical wintering ranges further dislocates birds. Species with strict habitat requirements return to the tropics to find smoking ruins where there had been shady layers of rain forest. If habitat loss weren't bad enough, dangerous, residual pesticides such as DDT are often applied in tropical farmlands. In addition, small insect-eating birds are suffering losses from aggressive nest parasitism by two species of cowbird. Fostering local populations of wild birds through feeding and bird gardening, combined with a bird consciousness that supports conservation efforts worldwide, may be a force that is powerful enough to save our songbirds.

THE IMPORTANCE OF BIRD FOSTERING IN GREAT BRITAIN

Indeed, bird feeding and wildlife gardening are becoming increasingly crucial as song-bird populations in Britain decline due to the combined effects of habitat loss driven by population increase, introduction of heavy metals into waterways, and shifting of agricultural methods. The British Trust for Ornithology has recently published the results of a thirty-year common-bird census. Its disturbing results pinpoint several sources of loss. The use of herbicides that destroy seed-bearing weeds has eliminated a prime food source for skylarks, linnets, and corn buntings; the switch to sowing grain crops in autumn rather than spring has reduced the food supplies for birds during their breeding seasons; the loss of hedgerows due to modern "clean farming" practices has reduced breeding and feeding habitat of many species; and the rise of one-crop farms has reduced the diversity of food

Linnets are small, gregarious British finches whose stout beaks are specialized for grasping seeds and cracking the husks. Although linnets also eat insects, their summer menu includes waste seed left in farmers' fields and seeds of wild plants such as thistle, rape, flax, chickweed, and dandelion. In winter, they feed on berries, especially holly, ivy, and mountain ash.

sources available to British birds. It is estimated that in the countryside of the Midlands and the South, where agricultural changes are the most acute, hedgerows are disappearing from farms at the rate of more than one yard per acre per year. Hedgerows provide cover for nest sites and roosts and give protection from predators. While it is unlikely that artificial food sources will be able to compensate for drastic loss of habitat and climatic fluctuations, bird feeding may help weak individuals survive the rigors of winter. Bird fostering and the conservation attitudes it embodies will certainly help Britain's stressed wild bird populations to survive.

THE IMPORTANCE OF BIRD FOSTERING IN AUSTRALIA

Australia has many of the same problems seen in Britain and North America. Again, the unfortunate rule seems to be that human settlement destroys natural habitat, displacing and threatening some specialist birds, while increasing the numbers of other, more resilient species. Removing the cover of natural vegetation, as in mallee lands, has drastically altered the composition of bird populations, degradation of Australia's interior rangelands has led to massive soil erosion and silting up of natural waterholes, and complex natural habitats in tree plantations have been lost. The introduction of foreign predators such as the fox and house cat continues to decrease the numbers of Australian birds who haven't had enough time to evolve defenses against them.

The introduction of alien birds poses other problems for native Australian species. English settlers, lonesome for the comforting sights and sounds of "home" and not realizing the negative effects that British birds would have on the Australian avifauna, have settled twenty-one species of exotic birds in Australia. One of these, the European starling (*Sturnus vulgaris*), a notably aggressive and adaptable (some think nearly indestructible) species, is typical of the problem. Starlings compete with small, native parrots for nest holes, and because they are such aggressive birds, they oust the smaller birds from desirable nesting sites. These are usually at a premium, and it follows that many species of small, native parrots have had less

reproductive success because of the interference of starlings. No species of Australian bird has become extinct since 1788, but the night parrot (*Geopsittacus occidentalis*) has not been reliably reported for nearly fifty years and the paradise parrot (*Psephotus pulcherrimus*) is thought to be extinct. Australian ornithologists, however, have not given up on either bird yet. And there is reason for them to be hopeful. The noisy scrub-bird (*Atrichornis clamosus*), previously thought to be extinct in Australia, was rediscovered in 1961, and its habitat, Two People Bay near Albany in Western Australia, has been declared a reserve.

Because of the pressures on native Australian birds, providing food and water, nest boxes, and cat-free gardens filled with native food plants can make a difference in their continued success.

Starlings have been introduced in Australia and North America, much to the detriment of less aggressive native species. Although many people loathe starlings because a flock can quickly empty a backyard feeder, they are beautiful, lively birds whose plumage changes with the seasons: Their feathers are spangled with white tips in the winter and dark in the summer as the white tips wear away. One way to foil a flock of starlings is to feed early in the day, giving smaller, less aggressive birds a chance to feed before starlings arrive.

CHAPTER ONE

Water

Providing a constant supply of fresh water is a relatively simple way to attract a wide variety of birds to your yard. The bonus to the bird-watcher is that water will draw species who never visit feeders, especially insect eaters such as warblers and flycatchers, who hunt in the high canopy, and shy thrushes and vireos, who prefer densely shaded understory. There is even a report of screech owls visiting a birdbath. In much of Australia and arid portions of the United States and Canada, a birdbath will be the center of attention once the birds discover it.

AVIAN WATERING HOLE

As they make their daily rounds, birds continually scout for safe and appropriate watering holes, and although it probably won't be instantaneous, they will capitalize on water when you offer it on a regular basis. Birds visit baths for many reasons, but thirst is their primary motivation. We generally associate birdbaths with lush, blooming gardens and mild weather, but this is a misconception because birds are

thirsty year-round. They have three major sets of salivary glands and a variety of smaller ones to provide lubrication of the food they eat, but water is as important to their health as it is to ours. Because of the dry nature of their diet, seed and insect eaters tend to drink more water than fruit eaters do, but no matter what they eat, all birds need water.

THE BATH-FLIGHT CONNECTION

Bathing is an important feature of feather maintenance. A thorough soaking, followed by vigorous preening, re-oiling, and a shake in a dust bath, cleans and realigns the microscopic zippers that compose each feather. Thus, bathing helps keep plumage in top-flight condition. Care of feathers probably means the difference between life and death, because feathers not only make flight possible but also insulate the bird from extremes of heat and cold. Bathing allows birds to cool off on hot summer days and perhaps relieves the itch and irritation of mite and feather-louse infestations. Birds seem to bathe most in August and September, when they are molting, but many birds even take a dip in cold weather.

HOURS OF ENTERTAINMENT

Watch birds at a bath for even a short time and you're sure to laugh at their hilarious antics and ridiculous postures. They vigorously splash, duck, shake, wriggle, and preen; some seem to enjoy themselves as much as children do playing in the sprinkler, while others seem furiously indignant at their mop of soggy, disarranged feathers. Once your birdbath is accepted by the birds, you will be able to observe different species' bath routines. And, if you provide a dust bath, you'll see a waterless version of the same set of postures.

Providing a supply of fresh, safe water will draw birds that would otherwise ignore your backyard.

Your birdbath may be the only convenient and clean puddle of water for miles. Bathing antics such as these are your reward for maintaining your birdbath in pristine condition.

BATH ROUTINE

Once a bird has waded into the water, it typically squats down and fluffs its feathers. It flicks its wings in and out of the water, sending up fountains of spray. Then it wets its breast feathers and submerges even deeper, rocking its body back and forth to slosh water onto its back and douse its tail feathers. If you watch carefully, you will see it alternately transform into a feathered pincushion and then a scrawny, slicked-down bird as it repeatedly lifts and lowers all of its feathers. Presumably, this action allows water to penetrate to the skin as well as draws each feather through the water, removing oil and dirt. Rolling and submerging will be repeated, along with much wing pumping and neck dipping, until the bird is completely saturated and looks like an animated dishmop. It will then shake itself like a wet dog, sending droplets flying in all directions, and hop out of the water and onto a convenient perch to preen, oil, and rearrange its feathers.

HOW DEEP AND HOW HIGH?

If you watch birds as they bathe in the wild, you'll notice two things: First, they keep to shallow water, and second, their feathers get so wet that many can hardly fly after a luxurious soak. These observations tell you nearly everything you need to know about birdbaths; the watchwords are *shallow* and *safe*.

Because they drown easily, land birds avoid deep pools. Their cousins—penguins, loons, gulls, petrels, ducks, geese, swans, and others—have specially adapted feet to help them paddle efficiently. Their well-oiled feathers let them float like corks. Land birds, in contrast, have slender toes that are specialized for perching or hopping but are useless for swimming. Swifts, swallows, martins, and hummingbirds have the weakest, smallest feet of all. Consequently, they don't even enter the water, preferring to bathe on the wing or in spray from waterfalls (lawn sprinklers are a substitute that is readily accepted by hummingbirds). Woodpeckers have even stranger bathing habits. They never go to water holes, but instead perform all the postures of the bathing routine in wet leaves.

FEAR OF THE DEEP

Most land birds seem to have an instinctive fear of deep water and go into lakes and ponds only as far as the margins. They prefer shallow puddles of rainwater or places where creek or river water barely slides over stones. Your birdbath should mimic these natural conditions. There should be only two to three inches (5.2 to 7.7cm) of water in the bath, and the water should gradually slope to this maximum. Make sure that the birds have only a half inch (1.3cm) of water where they enter. In addition, if your bath has both deeper and shallower portions, both large and small birds will be able to use it. If you must use a container with steep sides, use large, flat stones to create the shallow stretches of water that backyard birds are most comfortable with.

ROUGHENED SURFACES

All birds will feel more secure if they can bathe and drink without losing their balance. In addition, they should be able to leap up to safety in a moment, without slipping. Make sure that your birdbath has a roughened surface for good traction. If you are using an improvised plastic or other slippery tub, adhesive, anti-slip appliqués will give the birds good footing.

LOCATION

Safe is the watchword here. Waterlogged birds are poor flyers and easy marks for cats that lurk in shrubbery, waiting to snatch a mouthful of wet bird. The ideal birdbath will be free of shrubs for twenty-five feet (7.5m) and have low overhead branches for escape cover. The overhanging branches will serve two other functions: They will shade the water and keep it cooler at midday and will also screen bathers from the aerial predators who will soon learn that potential prey is splashing in your birdbath.

Suspending a birdbath helps eliminate places for predators to hide and stalk vulnerable, wet birds. If you try this alternative to a more traditional pedestal birdbath, choose a place that has some branches nearby to provide perches for waiting birds and shelter where freshly bathed birds can groom themselves in safety.

A ground-level bath will be popular with many species. Here, a female house finch tests the water.

If your yard has no suitable shaded spot, the birdbath can be placed in the open, but this will limit its clientele to birds that feel safe in open, sunny areas. Shy, shade-loving birds will ignore a bath in an exposed location.

Finally, you will want to place your birdbath in a spot that is convenient for comfortable viewing as well as within reach of your garden hose. Perhaps the worst place to put a birdbath is near your bird feeders. Seeds, hulls, and droppings will foul the water in a short time, making an unsightly and unsanitary mess that birds will avoid.

PEDESTAL OR GROUND LEVEL?

Pedestal baths are not only more graceful, they are also safer if cats are a problem. Birds, however, seem to prefer bathing in a more natural situation: on the ground. You might combine the two by using a pedestal bath with a ground-level bath below it. This is especially effective if a drip bucket is suspended above the pedestal bath and if the overspill from the pedestal bath is set up to plink down into the ground-level bath.

One of the most convenient pedestals is a hollow plastic design. You unsnap the bottom and fill the pedestal with sand or dirt. A plastic pedestal has the advantage of being lightweight and easier to move about the garden. A plastic birdbath is much less expensive than a cement one, and it will not crack if the water in it freezes, which, unless you live in the tropics, is bound to happen sooner or later.

Do-it-yourselfers can make their own bird pools by digging a hollow in the ground. Its size and shape will be dictated by individual taste, but the same rules apply: The finished pool should be no more than three inches (7.7cm) deep and should gradually grade to this maximum depth. The earth should be covered with black plastic sheeting, then wire netting should be molded over the sheeting to keep the cement pool from cracking. A homemade cement pool can be landscaped to look very natural and has the advantage of being able to accommodate whole flocks of bathers. It will require daily hosing to remove windblown debris, but the birds will love it.

Pedestal birdbaths also come in handsome ceramic saucers that can be either mounted on a pole or hung. Both look as though they would work well, but because they are so shallow, all it takes is a single, vigorous bather to empty one of these and the birder will have to spend the entire day tending the bath. In addition, most ceramic saucers that I've seen in use have been broken—either by ice or by accident. Their susceptibility to freeze breakage is a major drawback.

DRIPPING DEVICES

Try rigging up some sort of dripping device in your birdbath; the sound of moving water will act as a bird magnet. The simplest device is a pail with a tiny hole punched in its bottom so that a drop falls once or twice a second. Keep in mind, however, that the container should hold at least a day's supply of dripping water and that only a minute hole is necessary—not even the most devoted birder has the time to continually refill an empty drip-bath bucket throughout the day. A drip bottle, large coffee can, ample construction bucket, or similar container suspended several feet above the bath are all worth trying, although some experimentation will be necessary before your system works perfectly. A lid on the bucket will reduce evaporation, and a pulley will help you raise and lower the bucket with ease. You may also want to paint the bucket to hide it or even use hot glue to attach plastic fern fronds or silk leaves.

An alternate, inexpensive method to providing a drip is to use a garden hose, but unless you have a plethora of out door spigots, this will not be a practical solution to supplying that noisy drip to your birdbath. To make your drip bucket noisier, experiment with the range of sounds produced by a drop falling into canisters of various heights. A tall can should advertise your birdbath with a resounding and audible *plink*, which will be irresistible to the birds.

There are many stylish commercial drip fountains available; all of them seem to work well and all of them will help birds find your birdbath. They will save you time and may look much neater than the drip bucket you construct from the odd bits that are tucked into your garage or basement. Consult any issue of *Wild Bird* or *Audubon,* or see the sources listed at the end of this chapter. Because they run on electricity, most commercial drip fountains are best suited for patios or decks, where they can bring views of bird behavior just about onto your breakfast table.

© Richard Day

The design of this drip bucket makes it pleasing to human eyes, while the plink of water into the birdbath below makes it attractive to avian ears.

KEEPING IT CLEAN

The only negative aspect of providing a birdbath is the grind of daily maintenance. Birds are notoriously messy, and windblown debris quickly accumulates in birdbaths and fouls the water. A dirty birdbath is a breeding ground for bacteria and algae, and both of these may pose health hazards to birds. In addition, birds shun dirty water. Once you begin to supply water to the birds, it becomes a daily obligation, but the fun of watching birds in their bath more than compensates for the drudgery involved.

The easiest way to fill and clean birdbaths is to use a strong jet of water from your garden hose. About once a month, you should scrub the bath with bleach or detergent to control algae and slime.

© Richard Day

Although this backyard setup is far from elegant, it supplies an overhead drip that doesn't require frequent refilling.

A long-handled brush works quite well and can be tucked into your bird cart to make the job easier (see chapter 6, page 70). Make sure to rinse all traces of cleaning agent from the birdbath before you refill it.

© Christopher Bain

The simplest way to offer birds a spot for summertime bathing is to fill the lid of a metal garbage can with fresh water daily.

A birdbath makes a lovely embellishment to any garden.

WHAT TYPE IS RECOMMENDED?

There is no perfect birdbath. Ceramic and terra-cotta are prettiest, but they'll shatter if they're dropped or knocked over, and a sudden freeze will crack them. Cement is strong and can support the weight of water, but cement is terribly heavy and it also cracks from freezing. Plastic is lightweight and won't be damaged by freezing, but if it isn't weighted down, it can be tossed about by the wind as well as by vigorous bathers. In addition, since we all want to reduce the amount of plastic in our lives, it's not very green to use plastic bird products, but sometimes there is no viable alternative. In freezing weather, only plastic works well because it endures extreme temperatures. Metal garbage-can lids turned upside down make great baths for summer, but cold metal is uncomfortable for human hands and doesn't work well in winter. Homemade poured-concrete ground pools are probably the best all-around birdbaths, but they are only practical if you have a large yard or garden.

WINTER BIRDBATHS

Birds probably need access to water more in winter than they do in summer, because local sources of water are often frozen for months at a time. Dehydration can be a major problem. To make matters worse, processed birdseed may have less moisture than wild foods do. When the landscape is frozen and snow-covered, birds will resort to eating snow to get the water they need, a habit that robs them of body heat. Birds who have access to fresh water don't have to waste body heat to melt ice or snow, which ultimately enhances their chances for survival.

There are several sorts of winter birdbaths, but all will be used mainly for drinking. In harsh winter weather, birds seem to know that it is potentially life threatening to bathe as often as they do in more temperate weather. The simplest winter birdbath is a shallow saucer of hot water that can be offered somewhere near your bird feeders but not close enough to become filled with seed and hulls. The disadvantage of a saucer of hot water is that it will quickly cool

Courtesy of Duncraft, Inc.

A clear plastic birdbath mounted on a high pole and set within viewing distance of your favorite easy chair can provide fascinating glimpses into the private bathing habits of your favorite backyard visitors. If you try a model like this and the birds avoid it, dry the bath and apply concentric rings of clear silicone cement to the inside to give the birds' feet something to grip while they bathe.

Courtesy of Allied Precision Industries; Photography by Tom Crawley

Birds need water, especially when most natural sources have frozen. The heated water you provide will increase the number and diversity of your backyard pensioners.

and eventually freeze, necessitating a series of trips to the feeder area to refill it. Immersion heaters are a more expensive solution to offering a constant supply of fresh water in cold weather, but make sure to use a heavy-duty outdoor extension cord and follow the manufacturer's directions to the letter so that no one receives a nasty jolt. There is also a solar birdbath on the market, which eliminates the need for electricity and its potential hazards. The solar bath is about as expensive as the immersion heaters, but well worth trying.

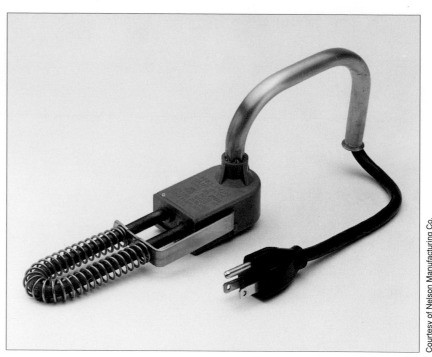

Courtesy of Nelson Manufacturing Co.

Don't let the looks of this immersion heater deter you. When properly connected to an outdoor extension cord, it is safe for birds, people, and pets.

The bargain-basement alternative to purchasing an expensive immersion or solar cold-weather birdbath is to use a heating unit that sets a light bulb below the saucer of the birdbath. The drawback to this method is that the bulb does not generate enough heat to keep the water from freezing at sub-zero temperatures. Winter baths will need daily attention, so placement that is convenient for the birder is crucial.

SOURCES OF SUPPLY FOR BIRDBATHS

CERAMIC BIRDBATHS

Opus Blue Bowl
OPUS
P.O. Box 525
Bellingham, MA 02019

TERRA-COTTA BIRDBATHS

Leaf Birdbath and Green-Glazed Birdbath, Hanging or Standing
GARDENER'S EDEN MAIL
ORDER DEPARTMENT
P.O. Box 7307
San Francisco, CA 94120-7307
1-800-822-9600

Terra-cotta Birdbath
SMITH & HAWKEN
25 Corte Madera
Mill Valley, CA 94941
(415) 383-2000

PLASTIC BIRDBATHS

Garden Scene Bath
DURACO PRODUCTS, INC.
Available in chain stores such as Walmart across the United States.

Universal Water Dish
OL' SAM PEABODY CO.
109 N. Main Street
P.O. Box 316
Berrien Springs, MI 49103
(616) 471-4031

IMMERSION HEATERS

Nelson Birdbath Heater
("Blue Devil" Model 30204, "Cedar Line Heated Birdbath," and Olio Birdbath Heater)
NELSON MFG. CPO.
3049 12th Street SW
P.O. Box 636, Dept. W.
Cedar Rapids, IA 52406
(319) 363-2607

Oasis Birdbath Heater
AUDUBON WORKSHOP
1-800-322-9464

SOLAR BIRDBATHS

Solar Sipper ("Model STDSS Solar Black")
HAPPY BIRD CORP.
479 South Street
Foxboro, MA 02035

DRIP BATHS

"The Deck Oasis" with "Oasis Dripper" or the "Stand-by Oasis"
AUDUBON WORKSHOP
1-800-322-9464

"The Dripper"
OL' SAM PEABODY CO.
109 N. Main Street
P.O. Box 316
Berrien Springs, MI 49103
(616) 471-4031

An immersion heater keeps the water in this roomy, concrete birdbath warm and allows it to be used in the winter, without worry that freezing water will crack it. This method is not advised if winter storms disrupt your electric service.

CHAPTER TWO

Planning Your Feeding Area

THINK LIKE A BIRD

You've got to think like a bird to plan a successful bird-feeding area. Most people don't realize that although the kind of food in the feeder is important, the design and placement of your bird feeders will drastically alter the feathered clientele who frequent your yard. Although we tend to think of birds as free-flying spirits, birds are actually quite rigid in their feeding habits. Backyard birds ordinarily include seed, fruit, and insect eaters as well as nectar sippers, but only a handful of species are omnivorous. Common crows, jackdaws, pied currawongs, blue jays, and grackles are exceptional in the wide spectrum of foods they eat, but an Anna's hummingbird will starve to death surrounded by sunflower seed. A brambling scorns all food except insects, while hawfinches prefer large, tough seeds. Birds also specialize in feeding in different strata of vegetation, and this affects their behavior at bird feeders. For example, doves are ground feeders who never cling to hanging feeders; woodpeckers (except the northern flicker) seldom feed on the ground, preferring suspended vertical or horizontal suet feeders; many birds prefer to hunt for insects in the highest treetops and are never drawn to seed feeders; while the vast majority of seed eaters prefer their table to be set about five feet off the ground.

DECISIONS, DECISIONS

Because few homes are designed with bird feeding in mind, the initial planning of your feeder area may present problems. Most houses look inward; they are made to be seen rather than for seeing. You may find that your home doesn't have a perfect place for bird feeding and bird viewing, and like most people, you'll be forced to improvise. As you visualize your bird-feeding area, keep in mind that it must combine these features.

1. It should be visible from your favorite chair (or a comfortable substitute), because once the birds start arriving, you will want to sit and watch them.
2. It should be sufficiently private as birds have terrible table manners and you don't want their mess to detract from the appearance of your property.
3. It should be protected from cold winds.
4. It should offer cover where birds can escape from predators, but it should not be so close to bushes that it becomes a cat-feeding area.

This mountain chickadee is feeding from a mugful of homemade bird treat. The coated wire provides a secure perch, and the small size of this feeder may spark ideas of how to devise a winter feeder that will bring birds right to your window.

© Kent & Donna Dannen

5. It should be easily accessible for servicing of feeders in freezing weather.

Also remember that if you have snowy winters, you must plan how snowdrift, snowfall, and snow-shoveling patterns will alter the accessibility and safety of your feeder area.

TO POLE-MOUNT OR SUSPEND — THAT IS THE QUESTION

Backyard bird feeders are typically suspended from tree limbs or are mounted or suspended from free-standing poles or posts. Before you decide on any of these options, consider the squirrel populations in your neighborhood, and take into account that an average gray squirrel can leap spans of eight to nine feet (2.4 to 2.7m), can shinny up unprotected metal poles, can scamper across electrical lines, and can leap four to five feet (1.2 to 1.5m) off the ground to raid your birdseed. Squirrels are a force to be reckoned with. They scare off the birds you want to attract and monopolize your feeders; they will even gnaw and destroy most wooden and plastic feeders. (See chapter 10 for more information on squirrels.) Even if there are no squirrels in your backyard right now, rodent intelligence is ever vigilant, and the local bushy-tails will soon learn that your backyard has a store of yummy goodies. An unprotected feeder is a potential squirrel diner, so it is better to include them in your initial plan. Some experts are so wary of squirrels that they advise against hanging a feeder from any tree, favoring baffle-defended, freestanding metal poles exclusively.

The branches added to this hopper feeder (above left) give birds such as this black-capped chickadee places to land, while the baffle keeps marauding cats and opportunistic squirrels away. The value of perches on a hopper feeder (above right) becomes obvious when viewed from this angle. Because of their strategic location, perches allow birds to feed while excluding their droppings and keeping the feeder clean. If you choose a wooden pole to support your feeder and don't add a baffle, however, you will soon be host to neighborhood cats, squirrels, and even raccoons.

POLES: METAL VERSUS WOOD

Let's face it: There is nothing pretty about the metal poles that are typical of backyard bird feeders. They are functional but hardly objects of aesthetic beauty. The advantage of metal poles over wooden posts is that metal does not rot and its slick surface makes attacks by cats, raccoons, opossums, and squirrels more difficult. Wooden posts can be made more attractive; they are also more expensive. Because of their more permanent nature, wooden posts are also a poor choice for the beginner, who will probably need to move a bird feeder several times before finding the perfect site. While most mammals can easily climb wooden posts, metal poles are a more difficult but not insurmountable challenge. A metal pole greased with petroleum jelly will provide you with some burlesque laughs as your backyard nemeses take a few pratfalls, but swipes of squirrel fur remove grease nicely, and this hilarious method of squirrel defense will be short-lived. You might try flavoring your anti-squirrel grease with cayenne pepper to further deter them, but this, too, will be only a temporary solution.

BAFFLES

Baffles, large cones constructed of an ungnawable metal and mounted below a feeder, provide the best defense. If you can't find any commercially made metal baffles in your area (and if you don't have a specialty birding or garden store in your area, metal baffles will be difficult to locate), anyone who is handy with tools can make a large and effective baffle by following the instructions on the next page. The size of your baffle will be governed by the size of your pole and feeder, but it is better to have a larger, rather than a smaller, metal baffle below your feeder. So that squirrels don't just leap above the baffle, mount it four and a half feet (1.35m) above the ground. Be prepared to move it higher if your squirrels are exceptionally athletic.

Wooden posts can be defended with metal baffles, too, but the combination of metal baffle and metal pole looks nicer than most metal baffles I've seen on wooden posts. The latter seldom go together and always seem as mismatched as hiking boots worn with an evening gown. In addition, some metal poles come with multiple arms, allowing you to concentrate several feeders in one spot, making viewing and servicing easier.

This attractive baffle comes with its own hardware, which makes it easy to attach to a pole. The only potential problem with this baffle is its material: Because it is not made of Lexan, squirrels will be able to gnaw their way through it to feast at your feeder.

PLASTIC BAFFLES: CAVEATS

Plastic baffles, designed to swivel beneath the weight of a marauding squirrel and tip the animal down to the ground, have the advantages of being lightweight and attractive as well as easier to find than metal baffles. If they work, plastic baffles disappear into the landscape while they protect suspended feeders from squirrels and rain. Their disadvantages center around the material that they're made of. Unless it's Lexan or another heavy-duty polycarbonate plastic, squirrels will gnaw through it to get to the birdseed beyond.

MAIL-ORDER SOURCES OF BIRD POLES

Unless you are a do-it-yourselfer, finding a pole for mounting bird feeders may be a problem. There are several mail-order sources (for example, Heath Manufacturing Company, P.O. Box 105, Coopersville, MI 49404-1239, 1-800-678-8183 and Ol' Sam Peabody Co., 109 North Main Street, P.O. Box 316, Berrien Springs, MI 49103, 616-471-4031) that will send alogs. In them, you will find less expensive triple-hanger poles and more elegant—and more expensive— wrought-iron poles with a pair of arms. If you want to hang more than three feeders, there are less expensive galvanized poles that come with ground sockets and mounting plates. Optional cross arms are available for these.

When buying a metal pole, perhaps the best solution is to buy one that comes with a ground socket. At your

This baffle will be effective—at least for a while, depending upon how intelligent and athletic your squirrels are—but try placing yours farther up the pole so that most squirrels won't be able to leap over it in a single bound.

feeder site, dig a hole and sink the ground socket into a plug of concrete. When this has dried, slip the pole into the socket. If you decide to move your feeder, just remove the pole and put in a new socket at the new location. The unused socket can be filled with soil.

HOW TO MAKE A BAFFLE

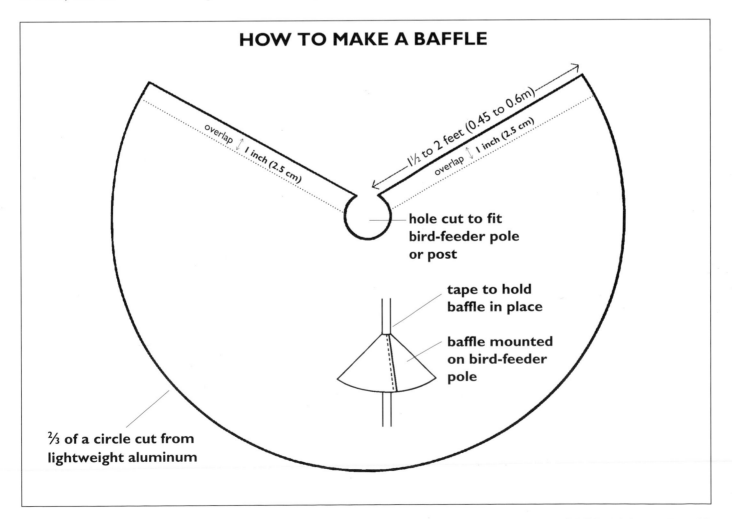

overlap ↕ 1 inch (2.5 cm)

1½ to 2 feet (0.45 to 0.6m)

overlap ↕ 1 inch (2.5 cm)

hole cut to fit bird-feeder pole or post

tape to hold baffle in place

baffle mounted on bird-feeder pole

⅔ of a circle cut from lightweight aluminum

DOING IT YOURSELF: POLES

With a few tools, the intrepid do-it-yourselfer can make a perfectly serviceable metal pole from supplies purchased at most hardware stores. The pole should be long enough to allow the lowest feeder to be five feet (1.5m) off the ground. Depending upon the weight it must support, galvanized pipe measuring a half inch to one inch (1.2 to 2.5cm) in diameter is suitable. If you are planning multiple feeders concentrated in one spot, the larger diameter is preferable. The upper end of the pole can be threaded to fit into a socket that will be screwed onto the underside of one kind of feeder. With a little ingenuity, metal arms such as those used to suspend hanging plant baskets can be adapted to fit securely around this pole. Thus, it is possible to support five or more feeders from one securely mounted, one-inch (2.5cm) -diameter pole.

THE SEVEN BASIC FEEDERS

• A ground-level platform for ground-feeding species.

• A platform feeder to attract species that feed in low brush; some of these will be skittish about alighting on the ground-level platform.

• A hopper feeder placed five feet (1.5m) off the ground to draw seed eaters.

• A tubular feeder filled with sunflower seeds to act as a magnet for finches, a tubular feeder filled with safflower seeds to attract finches and cardinals, and a thistle feeder filled with Niger seed to attract goldfinches.

• A suet feeder to attract woodpeckers, nuthatches, and a variety of insect-eating birds, which can be suspended high or low as well as nailed to tree trunks for bark-gleaners, such as creepers and nuthatches.

• A nectar feeder to draw hummingbirds and (if you are lucky) orioles and tanagers.

• Fruit feeders to attract orioles and tanagers.

ONE IS NEVER ENOUGH

As you gain experience, you'll learn that one feeder is never enough, so don't be deterred from putting out your second feeder. A period of experimentation will follow, during which you, a willing pupil, will be tutored by your backyard birds in the art and science of offering the foods they want when, where, and how they want them.

It will quickly become apparent that you will need several different kinds of feeders to attract the widest variety of species.

GROUND FEEDERS

Ground or platform feeders filled with cracked corn and mixed seed will attract all sorts of seed eaters, including pigeons, doves, ducks, pheasant, quail, geese, a variety of sparrows, and some finches. The best ground feeder drains water easily and has a lip all around the edge to prevent seed from blowing away. Larger is better than smaller: Three feet by four feet (90 by 120cm) should be a minimal size. Scour your basement or the local dump for something to use as a ground feeder. My all-time favorites are discarded window or door screens, held a few inches off the ground by cement blocks and weighted down with rocks. The biggest problem with ground feeders is that the food gets wet (and soon moldy) whenever it rains. But if you keep them clean, the birds seem to love screens, and the uneaten, spoiled seed can be easily discarded before you scrub and hose down these ground feeders. Because they will catch seeds discarded by birds feeding above, ground feeders are especially effective when placed below suspended feeders. If you place them below suspended feeders, however, you are honor bound to see that they don't become fouled with bird feces.

PLATFORM FEEDERS

Also known as a bird table, the platform feeder is a raised, flat tray, with a lip all around. Many experts recommend this feeder design for beginners mainly because birds see food on a tray easily, and its visibility will lure them into your yard much more quickly than

© Richard Day

Bobwhite quail (above, at right) become quite tame and will visit your ground feeder, especially if you mimic their whistle. Blue jays (above, at left, and below) are beautiful additions to any feeder.

© Sam Fried/Photo/Nats

a hopper feeder filled with sunflower seeds. In addition, some birds prefer a platform feeder to any other. A platform feeder can be at any height but should be fairly large so that birds aren't crowded together. Two by three feet (60 by 90cm) is an excellent size to begin experimenting with. It can be a simple rectangle or any design that pleases the birder and can be made from any material sufficiently sturdy to hold up to wind and weather.

Like the ground feeder, the tray feeder should have a lip and many holes for drainage. You might want to use your tray feeder to experiment with offering foods other than birdseed. Orange halves that are speared so they stay in place, blocks of suet, chopped table scraps, baked goods, apple cores (seeds and all),

raisins, dried nuts (including dried seeds from squash and melons), or just about anything that you want to share with the birds (including dried fruits and shot glasses full of orange juice) can go onto a platform feeder.

If you want to experiment with the individual preferences of the birds in your backyard with the intent of concocting a blended birdseed that will eliminate all the wasted mixed seed that the birds usually kick out of the feeder, a platform feeder is the place to do it. Some sort of compartmentalized tray is needed. I have found that a silverware tray, picked up at a local flea market, works well, but if you are handy with tools, you could make a compartmentalized tray from scraps of wood. Put a different kind of seed in

BLUEBIRD TREAT

$1/2$ cup oil (bacon drippings, rendered suet, lard, and recycled vegetable oil are all fine)
$2 1/2$ cups yellow cornmeal (not the expensive kind)
$1 1/2$ cups flour
2 tsp. baking powder
1 tsp. baking soda
$3 1/2$ cups milk or water
$1/2$ cup chopped nuts, dried raisins, peanut butter, chopped apple, or chopped carrots

Preheat oven to 350°F (180°C). Grease your baking pans. Oblong or square pans work best, but pie pans can also be used. Combine dry ingredients and mix thoroughly. Liquefy the shortening and add it to the mixture along with the milk or water. Stir in nuts (or one of the other ingredients) and pour the mixture into greased pans and bake for 40 to 50 minutes or until the bread is lightly browned. Put it into a mesh onion bag or suet holder to keep the larger birds from flying away with chunks of it. Extra can be stored in the refrigerator or frozen.

PEANUT BUTTER CONES

Peanut butter, bacon drippings, and birdseed are the basic ingredients in this concoction that attracts a wide variety of birds when it is smeared onto and into pinecones (children like to do this) and then offered at the bird table. Variations include rolling the filled pinecones in birdseed mixtures, using rendered suet instead of bacon drippings, and adding other treats to the mixture. Bread crumbs and crushed stale baked goods are two favorites. Graham crackers and dog biscuits ground in a blender will add extra nutrition.

SANDY DOGS

If you have a dog and cooking scraps (leftover pasta is perfect), your children may want to try this no-cook recipe.

1 cup crushed dog bones or dry kibble
1 cup sunflower seeds or wild-bird food
1 tbsp. sand
2 tbsp. peanut butter
$1 1/2$ cups rendered suet

Spoon the blended mixture into greased muffin tins, and pour $1 1/2$ cups rendered suet over the dry ingredients. Put the muffin pan into the freezer to set the individual "dogs." When they are firm, wrap each in a mesh bag (recycled onion or fruit bags are fine) and hang them all from tree branches.

Adding suet feeders to your hopper feeder increases the variety of species you attract. Here, a red-bellied woodpecker and a downy woodpecker feast on suet. Red-bellied woodpeckers seem to have a broader diet than many of their strictly insectivorous relatives. In the southern United States, they feed on sunflower seeds.

each compartment and keep track of what the birds prefer to eat. This assumes that a variety of seeds are available in your area or that you are willing to order them by mail. (See sources listed at the end of chapter 3, beginning on page 49.)

The platform feeder is also the place to try Bluebird Treat (see recipe on page 32) or to offer many of the mixes of food that you can cook up for birds, if you have a mind to. Platform feeders are also an excellent way to introduce children to birds and bird feeding. Children can try feeding birds almost anything on a platform feeder, and it would be worthwhile for a child (or a school class) to keep a record of the food preferences of various species. The rules to remember, though, are the same for any table set for birds: The food should be fresh and clean, and the feeder should

be checked daily and restocked regularly. While most mothers are too busy to cook for the birds, this is an excellent project for children (see instructions for Peanut Butter Cones and Sandy Dogs on page 32). It has the added bonus of teaching responsibility for living creatures and love and respect for nature.

HOPPER FEEDERS

In all its variations, the hopper feeder is the apparatus most people picture when you say *bird feeder*: a roofed box that is usually wooden, has two clear sides, and can be either pole-mounted or suspended. This model of bird feeder is the most popular, and there are many on the market. The advantage of a hopper feeder is that it keeps a quantity of fresh, clean, dry seed available. Birds peck at the seed that is accessible

FEATURES OF A HIGH-QUALITY HOPPER FEEDER

• It should be large enough to hold several pounds of seed.

• The material should be cedar, not pine.

• The top should move out of the way for easy filling.

• The roof should be leak-proof.

• It should be held together with brass screws, not with staples.

• The clear panels should be plastic, not glass.

• Look for a narrow gap for the seed to fall from the hopper out onto the platform below. If this gap is more than a half inch (1.3cm) from the hopper floor, small birds may be tempted to squeeze into the hopper and will panic and eventually die.

• It must have drainage holes.

• It should have a small perching area or attached perches so that birds cannot defecate into the seed.

This well-designed hopper feeder has a mammal excluder attached to the pole. This excluder will keep rodents at bay: As a mammal climbs up the pole, it enters the excluder, runs into a dead end, and has to retrace its steps.

through a narrow gap, and gravity keeps delivering seed until the feeder is empty. The major problems with wooden hopper feeders stem from dangers from bacterial contamination that are associated with them. Face it: There are probably only a handful of conscientious, superclean birders in the entire world who *regularly* scrub out their wooden feeders with bleach to disinfect them. Most of us are unaware or too busy, or we ignore the problem; at best, most of us give our feeders a once-a-season cleaning. The perfect solution would be a wooden feeder with a low-maintenance plastic flooring, but thus far, I have never seen such a product on the market. Until such a design is manufactured, however, you can make your wooden feeder safer for the birds by disinfecting it on a regular basis and altering its design

so that birds must perch to feed at the hopper. If this is impossible, it is worth experimenting with polyurethane plastic coatings that will keep fecal bacteria from multiplying in the interstices of wooden floors.

TUBULAR FEEDERS

Hanging tube feeders are made of plastic and have portals that dispense a gravity-fed flow of seed. Because birds cling to perches and peck seed from within the tube, fresh seed does not become contaminated with bird feces. Thus, while tubular feeders lack the charm of wooden feeders, they do eliminate the disease-spreading potential of wooden hopper and platform feeders. The clear plastic tube makes seed highly visible to birds, attracting them to your yard.

© Valorie Hodgson/Photo/Nats

FEATURES OF A HIGH-QUALITY TUBULAR FEEDER

• It should have seed baffles and metal portals that are less than one inch (2.5cm) in diameter to help control the flow of seed.

• It should be constructed of Lexan or poly-carbonate plastic, so it will not crack, succumb to squirrel teeth, break, or turn cloudy.

• There should be drainage holes in the bottom of the tube as well as in the bottom seed tray (if one is present) help keep the seed dry.

• The hanger should be attached not only to the cap but also to the tube to keep it secure.

• Look for a rain-proof metal cap that will slide up and out of the way to make refilling easy.

• Many tube feeders come with some sort of squirrel-proofing, often a metal mesh sleeve that is impervious to those ever-growing incisors.

Seed tube feeder courtesy of Aspects Inc.; Photo by Jim Messina

Hoppers and tubular feeders work by using gravity. By pecking at the opening of a feeder (top), birds remove seeds, and gravity pulls down others to replace them until the hopper is empty. Northern cardinals and a house finch (above) enjoy the rewards of a well-designed tubular feeder full of plump sunflower seeds.

A suet feeder provides birds with nutritious fats that are especially necessary on cold days. This feeder offers a commercial suet and seed block to a downy woodpecker.

SUET FEEDERS

Suet feeders are one surefire way to get insect-eating birds into view. Woodpeckers, titmice, chickadees, tits, nuthatches, mockingbirds, and starlings all love this source of animal fat. You can use something as simple as the netting from a bag of onions for your suet feeder or purchase a wire cage to suspend or nail horizontally or vertically to a tree trunk or limb. Suet

COLD-WEATHER METHOD FOR PREPARING SUET

Ask your butcher or supermarket for kidney suet (not "stringy" suet). Cut the fat into small pieces, chop it fine in a food processor, or have the butcher send it through his meat grinder. Melt the ground suet in a double boiler over low heat. Pour the melted fat into molds (muffin pans work well), and allow to cool and thicken before adding any seeds, berries, or other treats. You can add peanut butter, vegetable shortening, cornmeal, breakfast cereal, cooked rice, cooked noodles, flour, dried fruits and berries, ground bakery goods, leftover crackers, cracked corn, seeds, or even dried, finely ground meat to make a suet cake that the birds will relish.

WARM-WEATHER METHOD FOR PREPARING SUET

When the temperature rises above 70°F (21°C), suet prepared by the cold-weather method melts quickly, gets matted on birds' feathers, and tends to turn rancid. In warm weather, you should grind, heat, and cool suet as described above and then remove the solidified fat and allow it to cool. Then reliquefy the solidified suet, pour it into molds, and allow it to cool before adding any special ingredients. The second reheating drives off extra water and allows the suet to be much harder and less likely to melt and turn rancid in warm weather.

© Richard Day

The butcher at your local supermarket will usually save suet for you, especially when you make it known that you are feeding it to the birds.

is always offered in some kind of cage or bag for two reasons. First, you will want to keep large birds from carrying the precious morsel away to feed on elsewhere—usually up and out of sight. Second, you want to deter large birds, such as starlings and crows, from monopolizing the suet. A wire cage doesn't allow them to get more than a tiny bit at a time, while allowing smaller birds to eat relatively larger portions.

The suet you offer can be store-bought cakes or cakes that you prepare at home. In cold weather, you do not need to render the suet, but in the summer, when many people avoid feeding suet because suet melts above room temperature and turns rancid, you should use either suet cakes that are purchased rendered or rerender and harden it yourself.

Hummingbirds (above and below) lap up nectar with their long, tubular tongues. Hang a nectar feeder outside your window for close-up viewing of these high-speed fliers, and you'll be rewarded with insights into their lives as well as glimpses of hummingbird anatomy and behavior that are missed when the nectar feeder is hung far away. Watch for their transparent tongues. Try to see their feet and eyelids.

NECTAR FEEDERS

In the United States, especially in the South and West, sales of hummingbird feeders have skyrocketed. It seems that everyone loves these tiny, hyperactive birds, and feeding them is fast becoming a national obsession. Nectar feeders are inexpensive to buy and easy to fill and maintain. If hummingbirds are in your area, they will eventually find your feeders, claim them, and vigorously and vociferously defend them.

When you buy your first hummingbird feeder, you may be tempted to buy hummingbird nectar. Don't. Not only do you not need it, but it usually has red food coloring and other additives that the birds do not need and that may harm them. Hummingbird nectar appeals to busy folks who want to have a hummingbird feeder but don't want to make their own nectar. However, it couldn't be simpler. All you need is white sugar (not sugar substitute or honey) and water mixed one part sugar to four parts water. For example, mix one cup of sugar with four cups of water. Boil the

© C. Allan Morgan

Here, a hooded oriole perches at a nectar feeder. Note the size of the nectar openings.

WHEN YOU SHOP FOR A HUMMINGBIRD FEEDER, CONSIDER THE FOLLOWING DESIGN CRITERIA

• The more ports the better, especially if you live in the West or in the Caribbean, where there are more species of hummingbirds. My favorite feeders have six plastic perches to allow the birds to rest as they feed. Hummingbirds don't need to perch to feed—after all, they are the best fliers in the world and experts at hovering—but I like watching them at rest as well as in flight. Feeders with perches let the birds slow down to human speed, if only for a moment. They are also best for introducing children to hummers.

• Before buying a feeder, open the box and examine the internal structure of the feeder, keeping this question in mind: Can you reach every part of the feeder with a toothbrush? Hummingbird feeders are prone to developing a slimy, black fungus on all internal surfaces. Every time you refill your feeder, you are honor bound

to scrub its internal surfaces and remove this growth. The health of your hummingbirds literally depends upon your vigilance. What works beautifully for this task is an old toothbrush that's been bent in hot water until it has a forty-five-degree angle to the handle.

• Is the hanger secure?

• Is there a well around the hanger that you can fill with water to act as a moat to keep ants at bay?

• Because hummers are most attracted to red flowers, does the feeder capitalize upon that fact and feature red plastic on some part of the feeder?

• Look for a feeder with bee guards: small screens that keep insects at a distance from the nectar but allow hummingbirds' longer bills to reach the sweet stuff.

• To allow more than one hummer to use your feeder, look for plastic blossoms that are attached to the feeder to screen feeding hummingbirds from one another.

sugar water for about ten minutes to ensure that it doesn't ferment in your feeder. Allow the boiled sugar water to cool before pouring it into your newly scrubbed feeder. If you pour in boiling hot sugar water, a glass feeder will crack and a plastic one will be deformed.

FRUIT FEEDERS

Fruit feeders are only recently being marketed in the United States, mainly to attract orioles. If you are gadget mad or if you have a thoughtful gift-giving friend, you may end up with one of these plastic sleeves designed to hold half an orange securely. An alternative method to buying a fruit feeder is to spear orange slices—or halves of any fruit you'd like to try—on long nails driven up through the bottom of your platform feeder. If you don't have a platform feeder, spear fruit on leafless tree branches or tie it onto branches with string or monofilament. Once the birds have found your fruit offerings, you may want to make a fruit feeder by driving long nails through a piece of lumber and tying the fruit feeder (which will look like a miniature bed of nails) onto a horizontal tree limb (the dimensions of the lumber wlll be dictated by those of the tree limb).

A nicely designed fruit feeder will attract orioles to your backyard.

This bare-bones fruit feeder works just as well—perhaps better—as the commercial types, needs little maintenance, and never has to be taken in for the winter.

CHAPTER THREE

What Should I Feed the Birds?

You have now conquered two major obstacles in your quest to draw wild birds into your backyard: You have selected both a location and a feeder, and with any luck, your birdbath is in place and attracting birds to your yard. We must now turn to an infinitely more intricate subject: What do wild birds eat?

CONSULT THE LOCAL EXPERTS

There is one very easy way to find out what your wild birds will eat: Search out the wild-bird enthusiasts in your community. Every community, no matter how large or small, how urban or rural, contains a secretive cadre of enthusiasts who devote countless hours and dollars to feeding wild birds. The only problem is locating them. Some are as shy as brooding cardinals with a nestful of young, and many may prefer the company of their birds to that of humans, but everyone knows someone who feeds birds, and these are the resources you must cultivate. Consider their information carefully, however. While the advice of a local birder can save you a season of fruitless experimentation with foods that are scorned by the birds you want to attract, sometimes the experts are wrong.

BIRDSEED: THE MIX

Because most people buy their birdseed in bulk at large chain stores, supermarkets, or gardening centers, it follows that a commercial, mixed wild-bird seed is the most popular with wild-bird feeders. But is it most popular with wild birds? Most of us have little idea of the identity or nutritional value of the seeds in a typical bargain-bag mix, and because few seed companies have labels that tell you what sort of seed is inside the bag, I analyzed it to see what was being sold. If you have a supply of birdseed and a kitchen scale, you may want to spend a few hours sorting and weighing your mixed birdseed to get a better idea of what percentages of what seeds are being offered.

SUNFLOWER SEED

If you can identify any of the seeds in wild-bird seed, you will know this one. Sunflower seeds made up 10 percent of the grain in my wild-bird seed mix. There are two kinds: striped and black-oil seed. The striped seed comes in two varieties: black-striped and gray-striped. Both of these large seeds are used in candies and health-food treats like trail mix, and they're the seeds that produce the huge, ornamental sunflower plants. Black-oil seeds, on the other hand, are smaller, completely black-hulled, and are pressed to yield sunflower oil. While all three sorts of sunflower seeds are high in oils, fats, and proteins, the black-oil variety is richer and is preferred by the widest variety of birds. Titmice, chickadees, pine siskins, cardinals, evening grosbeaks, grackles, finches, and many sparrows prefer black-oil seed to both striped varieties. Because backyard feeding programs aim to foster excellent nutrition, a seed mix with a high percentage of black-oil sunflower seed will be best for the birds.

Gray-striped sunflower seed is a moderately priced favorite of many seed eaters.

Black-oil sunflower seed is the most preferred bird-feeder seed selected by the greatest percentage of feeder birds.

Its price prevents spray millet from being widely used in backyard bird feeders.

Of the 10 percent sunflower seed that I found in my bargain-bag mix, only half was the black-oil variety. I am currently experimenting with feeders filled exclusively with black-oil sunflower seed and suggest that you try it as a first choice, reserving the striped varieties of sunflower seed as a second choice. If you prefer to mix your own blend, add at least 50 percent black-oil and 20 percent striped sunflower seed.

CANARY SEED

This is the smallest seed in most mixes. It is a round seed with one slightly pointed end and has a glossy, yellow-white hull. While some birds will eat it, only mourning doves and song sparrows are really attracted to it. Nevertheless, it accounted for about 30 percent of the seed in my commercial mix. If I were blending my own backyard mix, I would avoid canary seed.

MILLET

If you separate canary seed from the other components and closely examine it, there will be a few seeds that look different from the others. Millet is a tiny, dull-looking yellow seed that has a conspicuous, dark speck on one side. It is a favorite food of many birds, including mourning doves, towhees, sparrows, juncos, cowbirds, and many ducks. There was so little millet in my sample of wild-bird mixed seed that I did not bother to weigh it, but my best guess is that only a small percentage was present, probably because millet is a fairly expensive grain, as compared with milo and canary seed. If you are concocting your own wild-bird food mix, include about 10 percent white millet.

MILO

This seed is also round, but it is twice the size of canary seed. It has a ruddy seed coat and is abundant in wild-bird seed mixes; it was the major ingredient in my commercial mix, accounting for 40 percent of my sample. Milo is the seed of sorghum, a crop that is grown for grain, syrup, fodder, and pasture food. Mourning doves and sparrows will eat it, although they prefer sunflower seeds and millet. I imagine that it is included in wild-bird seed because it is plentiful and cheap, but it is often discarded by wild birds.

BUCKWHEAT

This seed has a longitudinal split on one side, making it look like an elongated form of barley. It has a dull, light-brown seed coat and has little attractiveness to birds when compared with sunflower seed. It was also quite abundant in my wild-bird seed mix, accounting for 20 percent of my sample.

IS THE BARGAIN BAG A BARGAIN?

Everything is relative. Whether the inexpensive twenty-five-pound (11.25kg) bag of mostly undesirable seed is preferable to a twenty-five-pound bag of highly desirable black-oil sunflower seed at nearly twice the price depends upon the shopper's resources. Is it worth it to offer costly hulled sunflower seed (no hulls to leach grass-killing toxins into the soil—in fact, no mess at all), or should the birds husk their own seeds? Is white millet, an expensive seed, worth it? There is no doubt that inexpensive, mixed seed has a place in bird-feeding programs, but there are many species who will scorn your feeder if more attractive seeds are offered nearby. If the choice is between the bargain brand or no seed at all, however, the answer should be clear.

HOW SHOULD YOU FEED THE MIX?

Consider this scenario. Full of good intentions and overflowing with goodwill toward feathered creatures, our first-time bird feeder lugs a twenty-five-pound (11.25kg) bargain bag of mixed seed home from the local grocer, dutifully fills up the backyard hopper feeder, and settles back to watch. The birds arrive, but much to our bird feeder's dismay, some species reject the mixed seed, scattering it down onto the ground, where it becomes moldy or sprouts in the lawn. When the last sunflower seed is gone, the birds are, too. What should be done?

Apart from skirmishes with the ever-present squirrels, wasted seed is probably the most common problem faced by backyard-bird feeders. Some feathered guests (especially titmice) have picky appetites and kick out the varieties of seed that they don't like as they peck for their favorites. There are several strategies that will help you avoid this problem. You could open a cafeteria for the birds on a platform feeder (see chapter 2, page 30), offer them a wide variety of seeds, and let them show you which varieties of seed they prefer. If this seems like too much trouble, however (and for many people this will be impossible anyway, unless there is an exceptionally well-stocked feed and grain store nearby or you are willing to pay shipping costs), here are a few more suggestions.

- Use mixed seed and cracked corn in a ground or platform feeder.

- Use sunflower seeds (black-oil being the first choice, followed by the striped varieties) in a separate feeder.

- Offer thistle (see next section) in a third, specially designed feeder.

- Offer white millet in a fourth feeder.

OTHER ITEMS YOU WILL WANT TO TRY

PEANUTS AND NUTMEATS

If you have a ready supply of these on hand, chickadees, titmice, and jays will beat a path to your feeder. These usually don't make it to the bird feeder at my house—people eat them faster than birds do. Whole peanuts are taken by all species of jays and tits and by titmice, chickadees, and white-throated sparrows. Peanut hearts, which are infinitely more expensive, are favored by starlings.

© Dave McMichael

Peanuts are favored by jays, tits, and many other backyard visitors who don't mind shelling them to get at the nutritious meat inside.

GRIT AND CALCIUM

As your biology teacher once told you, birds have no teeth in their beaks and thus depend upon grit and small stones lodged in their gizzards to grind their food and make nutrients available for digestion and absorption. Birds need and appreciate any form of grit you provide. Sand and old mortar (probably because they are good sources of minerals) are special favorites and should be part of your feeding program year-round.

The platform feeder is a good place to offer both grit and ground oyster shells, which provide a wonderful source of calcium; a shallow wooden box nailed in one corner will do nicely. If you cannot find a source of ground oyster shells (usually sold at feed stores), you might collect eggshells, microwave them or bake them for about twenty minutes to kill any bacteria that might harm the birds, and whirl them in your food processor or otherwise fragment them. Birds need extra calcium in the spring and summer, when females are using their own reserves to produce eggs and young, but it is a welcome mineral supplement year-round.

NIGER (THISTLE)

When offered in specially constructed feeders, Niger or thistle seed is a favorite food of mourning doves, goldfinches, pine siskins, common redpolls, and house finches. Because thistle seed is so tiny, it must be offered in a specially constructed feeder. It is the most expensive feeder seed, but a little goes a long way. Make sure to protect your thistle tube from rain. In many backyards, thistle goes moldy before attracting any goldfinches.

Thistle seed is often called Niger seed because of its dark color. Members of the finch family such as goldfinches, purple finches, and house finches prefer it to most other feeder foods.

CRACKED CORN

There are two varieties of cracked corn: scratch feed. and baby-chick feed. Some birds seem to prefer the latter, probably because it is more finely ground and easier to eat and digest. Try whirling cracked corn in your food processor to convert it to a finer grind.

The reasons for the popularity of this feeder are clear: It has a wide baffle to foil furry competitors and predators, a seed tray to catch seeds rejected by feeders, ample perches and feed openings, and a secure rain cover to protect the seed. Most important to the birds, however, it contains plenty of high-quality seed.

Cracked corn will attract birds such as mourning doves, rock doves (pigeons), crows, starlings, juncos, grackles, house sparrows, ducks, and such fowl as quail, pheasants, and turkeys. Cracked corn is the least expensive of all wild-bird foods, so if you can't afford thistle, try grinding cracked corn fine and putting it into thistle feeders. Some people claim that the most desirable and colorful finches are attracted to it.

Cracked corn is a favorite of many ground-feeding birds. Try grinding it finely and serving it in your thistle feeder.

BUYING SEED

Depending upon where you live, a birding store, Audubon Workshop, or grain store may be your best source of supply for seed. Although a list of mail-order sources for bird foods follows, it is usually much cheaper to buy birdseed in bulk at a local source. If you live in a rural area, feed and grain stores may offer the best prices, but these vary dramatically, and you may want to invest some time in comparison shopping before investing your money. Bird clubs, garden clubs, church groups, and PTAs often raise funds by selling a specific blend of seed that local experts perfected. There is usually no waste in these blends.

OTHER SEEDS

• Safflower seed attracts cardinals, and it is worth offering in a separate feeder. If the birds ignore your safflower seed, mix it in equal proportions with sunflower seed and gradually reduce the proportion of sunflower seed. This may allow you to eliminate grackles and starlings from your hopper feeders.

• Flax, golden millet, sorghum, oats (whole and hulled), rice, rape seed, and wheat have a low attractiveness to most birds, so it seems a waste of time to try them in your feeders. They are, however, ingredients of some bargain-bag wild-bird mixes.

The design of this spherical feeder keeps out birds that are too large to cling to one of the small openings. Although it does discourage squirrels, it may not be completely safe for small birds—they may squeeze into the holes and become trapped within the plastic.

WILD-BIRD SUPPLIES

The following list is by no means exhaustive; these are the merchants of wild-bird feeding supplies that I am familiar with. Most have a catalog that they will send so you can comparison shop by mail. The dollar amounts in parentheses indicate the cost of the catalogs; those without a dollar amount supply catalogs for free.

NORTH AMERICAN SOURCES

General Stores

CHICKADEE
1300-L Wirt
Houston, TX 77055
(713) 956-2670
($1.00, refundable)

DUNCRAFT
Penacook, NH 03303-9020
(603) 224-0200

HEATH MANUFACTURING
COMPANY
P.O. Box 105
Coopersville, MI 49404-1239
1-800-678-8183

OLD ELM FEED & SUPPLIES
Box 57
Elm Grove, WI 53122
(414) 786-3304

OL' SAM PEABODY CO.
109 North Main Street
P.O. Box 316
Berrien Springs, MI 49103
(616) 471-4031

ONE GOOD TERN
1710 Fern Street
Alexandria, VA 22303
1-800-432-8376

WILD BIRD CENTER
101 Annapolis Street
Annapolis, MD 21401
(301) 280-0033

WILDBIRD COMPANY
617 Hungerford Drive
Rockville, MD 20850
(301) 279-0079

WILD BIRD SUPPLIES
Dept. WB
4815 Oak Street
Crystal Lake, IL 60012

YULE-HYDE ASSOCIATE LTD.
4 Lowry Drive
Brampton, Ontario L7A 1A3

Birdseed

BERKSHIRE FEED OUTLET
Box 317
Egremont, MA 01258
(413) 528-4967

BILL CHANDLER FARMS
RR 2 WB
Noble, IL 62868
1-800-752-BIRD

DAKOTA QUALITY BIRD FOOD
Box 3084
Fargo, ND 58108

GOLDEN BELT FEEDS
RR 1
Simcoe, Ontario N3Y 4J9

PRINCESS ANNE FARMERS'
SERVICE
5651 Virginia Beach Boulevard
Dept WB
Norfolk, VA 23502
(804) 461-1580
($1.00, refundable)

WILD BIRD CENTER
101 Annapolis Street
Annapolis, MD 21401
(301) 280-0033

Bird Feeders

BIRD WATCHER HOUSES &
FEEDERS
1866 Bell Road, WB
Nashville, TN 37217
(615) 366-6309

CARDINAL AMERICAN CORP.
4911 Grant Avenue
Cleveland, OH 44125
1-800-346-3425

SALT CREEK BIRDHOUSES
425 North Walnut
Dept. WB
Wood Dale, IL 60191
(312) 593-6791

VICTORY BUSINESS SERVICES
("The Aviarium" bird feeder)
9 Victory Lane
South Yarmouth, MA 02664
1-800-648-7254

NOTE: The staff at the Cornell Lab of Ornithology recently rated twenty-eight competing models of bird feeders. To obtain a free copy of this evaluation, send a self-addressed, stamped envelope to Crow's Nest Birding Shop, Cornell Lab of Ornithology, 159 Sapsucker Woods Road, Ithaca, NY 14850, or in Canada write to Long Point Bird Observatory, P.O. Box 160, Port Rowan, Ontario N0E 1M0. Ask for the Crow's Nest Catalog, too. It has many reference books and good prices on binoculars as well as bird-feeding supplies.

Birdhouses

ADIRONDACK ARTS AND
CRAFTS
P.O. Box 1
Wilmington, NY 12997
(518) 946-7476

COOSA RUSTICS
Route 1, Box 560
Rockford, AL 35136
(206) 377-2362

INTERESTING INVENTIONS CORP.
705 Algonquin Road
Rt. 62
Lake in the Hills, IL 60102

KINSMAN COMPANY
Dept. A63
River Road
Point Pleasant, PA 18950
(215) 297-5613

THE WOODPECKER SHOP
Route 3, Box 187
Dover, OH 44622

Purple Martin Houses

CARROLL INDUSTRIES
P.O. Box 577
Dept. WB
Madison, MS 39130

MR. BIRDHOUSE
2307 W. Highway 2 West
Grand Rapids, MN 55744
(218) 326-2362

NATURE HOUSE
1-800-255-2692

Societies and Newsletters

CARDINAL AMERICAN
CORPORATION
Advice for Bird Lovers
Cardinal Consumer Products
Division
4911 Grant Avenue
Cleveland, OH 44125

DICK E. BIRD NEWS
P.O. Box 377
Acme, MI 49610

NATIONAL BIRD-FEEDING
SOCIETY
1163 Shermer Road
Northbrook, IL 60062

NORTH AMERICAN
BLUEBIRD SOCIETY
Box 6295
Silver Spring, MD 20916

PROJECT FEEDERWATCH
Cornell Laboratory of Ornithology
159 Sapsucker Woods Road
Ithaca, NY 14850

Purple martin houses provide endless hours of entertainment as you watch the comings and goings at the openings to the "apartments." Be warned, however, that although martins dispose of enormous numbers of pesky flying insects for their human landlords, they are noisy, messy neighbors. Put the martin mansion far away from your own and everyone will be happy.

BRITISH SOURCES

Birdseed

ERNEST CHARLES & CO. LTD.
Freepost, Honiton EX14 8YZ
Tel.: (0404) 47020

HAITH'S BIRD FOOD
John E. Haith, Ltd.
Dept. BBC
Park Street
Cleethorpes DN35 7NF

Feeders

HENDON SQUIRRELS
(Squirrel-Proof Birdfeeder)
25 Sunningfields Road
London, Hendon NW4 4QR
Tel.: 081-960-0185

THE NUTTERY
42 Dene Road
Northwood, Middlesex
HA6 2DA
Tel.: (09274) 29592

Nurseries

BUCKINGHAM NURSERIES
45 Tingewick Road
Buckingham MK18 4AE
Tel.: Buckingham (0280) 813556

Native Wildflower Seeds

JOHN CHAMBERS
15 Westleigh Road
Barton Seagrave
Kettering, Northamptonshire
NN15 5AJ

EMORSGATE SEEDS
Terrington Court
Pope's Lane
Terrington Street
Clements, King's Lynn
Norfolk PE34 4NT

LANDLIFE WILDFLOWERS
The Old Police Station
Lark Lane, Liverpool L17 8UU

NATURESCAPE
Little Orchard
Main Street
Whatton in the Vale
Nottinghamshire NG13 9EP

SUFFOLK HERBS
Sawyers Farm
Little Cornard
Sudbury, Suffolk CO10 0NY

Societies

BRITISH TRUST FOR
ORNITHOLOGY
Dept. BBWW
The Nunnery
Nunnery Place
Thetford, Norfolk IP24 2BR

ROYAL SOCIETY FOR THE
PROTECTION OF BIRDS
Freepost
The Lodge
Sandy, Beds SG19 2BR

Books

HENRY SOTHERAN LTD.
2 Sackville Street
Piccadilly, London W1X 2DP
Tel.: 071- 439 6151
Fax: 071- 434 2019

SUBBUTEO NATURAL HISTORY
BOOKS, LTD.
Dept BBC
Fforrd y Llan
Treuddyn, Nr Mold, Clwyd
CH7 4LN
Tel.: (0352) 770 0581 (24-hr.)
Fax: (0352) 771 590

AUSTRALIAN SOURCES

Wild-Bird Supplies

BIRD OBSERVERS CLUB OF
AUSTRALIA
183 Springvale Road
Nunawading, Victoria 3131
Tel.: 03-877-5342
Fax: 03-894-4048

Societies

ROYAL AUSTRALASIAN
ORNITHOLOGISTS UNION
21 Gladstone Street
Moonee Ponds, Victoria 3039
Tel.: 03-370-1422
Fax: 03-370-9194

CHAPTER FOUR

City-Bird Feeding

Although my mother and sister have been bird-feeding enthusiasts for a long time, I resisted their efforts to convert me from bird-watcher to backyard-bird feeder for twenty years. To my mind, it was not nearly as pure as bird-watching, which requires a naturalist's specially honed skills as well as study, effort, sweat, and sometimes even blood, as you spend hours stalking tidal marshes and forest edges at dawn, hunting for those elusive warblers and baffling shorebirds. Besides, it seemed a moot point because I had no backyard; only four tiny rooms on the fourth floor of a New York City tenement that were crammed with too many books. Besides, even if I could find a local source for birdseed, how could I possibly carry those big bags up four flights of stairs, and where would I store them anyway? It all seemed impossible, messy, and not for me.

Then I moved out of my New York City apartment and settled in the Alabama countryside. Now, not only do I have a backyard, but there is a front yard, side yards, and acres of woodland with birds everywhere. So with this optimal bird-feeding environment at my doorstep—and with this book in mind—I set about learning to feed backyard birds. Now I recognize that there is a difference between feeder birds and the wild birds you see after patient stalking and careful observation in the field. Those you lure to your feeders become your birds as no birds glimpsed through binoculars can. As you watch your feeder birds, you observe their individual behaviors and learn the idiosyncrasies of various species that you can see only at close range. Watch

a chickadee flit into your feeder, select a single sunflower seed, and fly off to a perch. It will hold that seed between both feet and hammer at the hull with its bill. How does it manage to do this without falling off the branch? When the first seed is eaten, the

Even a city dweller can enjoy bird feeding. A tiny sunflower feeder attached to a window will allow you to adopt a sparrow.

A blue tit is feeding at this nicely designed window feeder. If this window is on ground level, however, it is only a matter of time before the cats and squirrels begin feeding here, too.

This narrow tray offers a chickadee-size banquet.

chickadee will be off for another and another and yet another sunflower seed until you have grown tired of watching. Birds are natural entertainers who enliven your garden—all for the price of a little birdseed and some water. Now I regret that I never fed the birds from my windows in Greenwich Village.

FOR THE CITY-BIRD FEEDER

Several problems face the city-bird feeder: where to put the feeder; where to get supplies; and how to get supplies with the least possible effort.

WHERE TO PUT THE FEEDER?

If you have no terrace, balcony, or even a postage stamp–size backyard, you should consider a window feeder. Here are several designs that will work.

1. A shelf with hoppers at either end will be secure and will not plummet to the pavement. The disadvantage of this design is that seed scattered on the shelf will attract doves and pigeons. Their noisy, rolling coos, the mess they create, and the breeding ground for aspergillosis their dung fosters will probably make this your least favorite design, especially if your apartment is small and the birds are intrusive. You can eliminate the disease potential if you scrub down the shelf regularly, sloshing a bucket of hot, soapy water onto it, and then make sure it is rinsed thoroughly.

2. Attach a bracket to your window frame and securely hang a tubular feeder to discourage pigeons and doves, but attract sparrows, chickadees, nuthatches, and finches. If you feed a premium feed such

as black-oil sunflower seed or hulled sunflower seed, there will be little mess to attract pigeons and no problem with wasted seed, while the bracket will keep your feeder from braining an innocent pedestrian.

3. An in-house window feeder, actually a variation of a terrarium that brings the birds right into your home, is the Rolex of shelf feeders. These have one-way glass, and the best have a wide wooden top that lifts to allow easy filling and cleaning. But these will not work for every city-bird feeder. You must have double-glassed frames that are twenty-four to twenty-seven inches (61 to 67cm) wide, as well as a good deal of money to purchase this feeder. If you are a do-it-yourselfer, you may be able to adapt the design of in-house bird feeders to your smaller windows by fitting panes of one-way glass into frames that will form the side panels and viewing screen of the finished feeder. The side panels attach to a wooden floor and a hinged wooden lid that lifts will provide easy access to the feeder platform.

4. The most conservative window feeder design and perhaps the one for a first-time bird feeder to try is a simple plastic feeder that attaches to the window with suction cups. There are several advantages to attaching your feeder to glass. Squirrels cannot reach it, and if it has a curved rain shield, pigeons will not be attracted to it or to the window sill below, especially if you feed hulled sunflower seed that has little wastage. When shopping for plastic, suction-cup attached feeders, keep these questions in mind.

• How easy is it to fill the feeder? If you have to climb about and do impossible contortions high above a metropolitan street when the feeder is empty, your enthusiasm for bird feeding may be dampened. The best small plastic window feeders lift out of their moorings to be filled within the house and replaced back outside the window.

• Is there a rain shield? Have provisions been made for drainage?

• What is the capacity of the feeder? Find one that holds at least two cups or more of seed.

• Can the birds see you? Mirrored film on the rear of the feeder will hide you from the birds and let you enjoy them at close range.

• How safe is the feeder for pedestrians on the street below? If you live on a busy street, it may not be wise (and may be illegal and irresponsible) to use a window-mounted bird feeder, because eventually, the suction cups will fail and your little plastic feeder will become a potentially deadly falling object. But don't let this deter you from trying a window feeder. You might glue the suction cups to a board that will be attached to the frame of your window or look for a feeder that will attach to your window frame with a clamp instead of suction cups.

SOURCES OF SEED SUPPLY

Because storage space is usually limited or nonexistent in apartments, the city-bird feeder will not be able to keep large stocks of birdseed on hand. One viable alternative is to order premium seed by mail and have it delivered to your door at regular intervals. For armchair comparison shopping, consult the list of seed suppliers in the previous chapter and send for their catalogs.

SOURCES OF IN-HOUSE WINDOW FEEDERS

Viewmaster
THE BROWN COMPANY
140 Dean Knauss Drive
Narragansett, RI
1-800-556-7670
($2.00, refundable on order)

Meta Magic Window
WILD BIRD CENTERS OF AMERICA, INC.
101 Annapolis Street
Annapolis, MD 21401
(301) 280-0033

U-View Bird Feeder
CEDAR WORKS
P.O. Box 266
Moorhead, IA 51558
(712) 886-5425

CHAPTER FIVE

Bird Gardening

One of the most effective means of attracting birds to your backyard is to use plantings to create a habitat that offers nutritious, natural food year-round as well as a suitable habitat for nesting and cover to escape predators. In essence, you want birds to be comfortable in your backyard, and the richer the foods you offer and the denser the cover, the more comfortable the birds will be and the more you will have. Setting up bird feeders and providing free lunch and water will draw birds to your backyard, but thoughtful plantings will invite nesting residents who will bring their fledglings to your feeder. Your plantings will also attract insect-eating birds who never visit feeders, and it follows that the greater the variety of trees, shrubs, vines, and wildflowers you plant, the greater the variety of birds that will be attracted to your yard. Here are some planting suggestions.

Cover. Between 8 and 15 percent of the trees and shrubs in your yard should be needle-leaved evergreens to offer birds shelter in cold, wind, and rain as well as sanctuary from prowling cats and diving raptors. If your trees and shrubs include equal proportions of broad- and needle-leaved evergreens and deciduous species, you will attract the widest variety of birds.

Magnets. Some tree and shrub species are magnets for wild birds, attracting insect- and fruit-eating birds

Evergreens provide cover, foraging and nesting territory, and food for many species of birds.

Beeches are not only magnificent throughout the seasons, but they also act as magnets for many species of birds. Their mast provides food for many species who aren't attracted to bird feeders, and their spreading branches offer cover and nesting sites.

who will not be drawn to usual feeder foods. Magnet trees include (in order from most to least attractive) mulberry, tupelo, hackberry, crab apple, oak, sassafras, sweet gum, beech, pine, walnut, elm, birch, maple, hawthorn, alder, ash, and hemlock. Magnet shrubs and small trees include cherry, sumac, serviceberry, holly, elaeagnus, dogwood, buckthorn, and juniper. Low shrubs and vines that are magnets include elderberry, blackberry, raspberry, blueberry, Virginia creeper, grape, bayberry, honeysuckle, viburnum, spicebush, bittersweet, rose, and barberry.

Bugs. If you can increase the attractiveness of your garden for bumblebees, butterflies, and a wide variety of beetles and beneficial flies, it will automatically be interesting to insect-eating birds. To increase the insects in your garden, one of the most important first steps is to create a pesticide-free zone. If you use artificial chemical poisons that will kill many harmless and beneficial insects as well as the few that you want to eliminate, stop using them. Use companion planting to help control pest insects: California poppy and French marigold among the vegetables will draw

hoverflies, whose larvae will attack greenflies. Aid ladybugs (ladybird beetles) by providing hollow plant stems for winter hibernation sites. If your climate is mild enough, insects will be present year-round in your garden if they have food supplies, particularly nectar and pollen. A shopping tip to keep in mind when selecting plants at a nursery is to buy those that are buzzing with bees, because individuals of a species vary in nectar and pollen productivity. In winter, nectar and pollen are at a premium: If your climate permits, try winter-flowering heather, *Erica camea*, *Crocus chrysanthus*, and grape hyacinth. In spring, honesty, broad bean, hyssop, and valerian are recommended, while in summer, yarrow, *Buddleia davidii*, and goldenrod are outstanding pollen and nectar producers. Michaelmas daisy and English ivy are good choices for autumn.

In spring, honesty's abundant pollen and nectar attract a plethora of insects, which in turn draw birds into your garden.

Hyssop (top) will draw bugs and birds, while large trees, such as an oak (above), provide foraging, feeding, and nesting territory for insectivorous birds and species that are too shy to come to bird tables.

Arrangement. It does little good to put magnet trees and shrubs—those that are irresistible to birds—in the back of your yard, where you cannot see them. Put them close to the house or deck or other convenient observation points.

Surroundings. Consider your garden as a bird might view it: as a piece of a larger landscape. For example, a bird might see the open lawns with scattered, small saplings as a short-grass prairie or plains. If you plant a thick wall of quick-growing shrubs or a tangle of vines, the birds may see your yard as an islandlike grove amid the grassland. In contrast, if the surrounding neighborhood is heavily wooded, your open lawn may be seen as a meadow. You might want to plant shrubs and flowers that will enhance this effect.

Edges. Birds like edges or transitions between habitats, and you should exploit edges to draw birds into your garden. Make sure your tree-shaded, thick plantings of understory shrubs and vines are visible from the house. If your yard has many dense beds of shrubs, consider uprooting some and replacing them with grass and beds of flowers to increase edges.

This small yard is packed with microhabitats that include water, flowering plants to attract insects, and cover for nesting and hiding from predators.

Flowering trees, such as this apple tree, provide a beautiful, versatile backdrop for your backyard birds.

Fruits are irresistible to humans and birds alike.

Messy. Don't be too meticulous in your garden. Birds seem to like a messy garden better than a painstakingly manicured one. Leave dead trees and stumps wherever possible to give cavity nesters and bark drillers breeding and feeding sites. If possible, leave leaf litter so that ground-dwelling species and those that hunt for insects and mollusks on the forest floor will have this resource.

Shade and sun. The open areas of your garden will attract birds who feel comfortable in the open, rather than in leaf shade. But if there are no trees in your yard, don't expect to lure shade-loving species of birds.

Weeds. Many birds are much more attracted to weed seeds than to tame garden plants, and an out-of-sight corner allowed to grow wild will be popular with birds. Gathering weed seeds is a fall project and one that is especially good for children. Gather seeds in fields and by the roadside by stripping handfuls of grass seeds and seeds of other desirable wild plants into a paper bag. Plant the seeds in a bed that is specially turned over for this purpose, but beware: In Britain, a weed corner that harbors "injurious" weeds such as ragwort, curled and broad-leaved dock, and spear and field thistles may reward the bird gardener with a fine from the local council or Ministry of Agriculture. In the North American "burbs," your neighbors may become incensed if your delightful weeds suddenly sprout in the middle of their perennial borders and zoysia grass.

Fruit. Plants and shrubs that have berries in cold weather will attract large numbers of birds. Birds relish berries of japonica, cotoneaster, berberis, holly, rowan,

Chaffinches (top) are fond of low-growing gorse bushes, whereas mistle thrushes (above) are especially attracted to berries.

hawthorn, pyracantha, stranvaesia, cherry, and viburnum. Can you offer an arbor that will eventually have enough grapes for you and the birds? It also helps to leave as many spent blossoms on plants as possible so that their seeds will ripen and provide bird food.

Flowers. Here is a list of annual and perennial plants that will provide flowers and seeds for birds: quaking grass (*Briza maxima*), love grass (*Eragrostis tef*), hare's tail (*Lagurus ovatus*), crimson fountain (*Pennisetum setaceum*), plains bristle grass (*Setaria macrostachya*), amaranthus (*Amaranthus* sp.), sunflower (*Helianthus*), California poppy (*Eschscholzia californica*), love-in-a-mist (*Nigella damascena*), pink (*Dianthus*), zinnia (*Zinnia*), aster (*Aster*), purple coneflower (*Echinacea purpurea*), scabiosa (*Scabiosa spectabile*), globe thistle (*Echinacea*), coreopsis (*Coreopsis*), butterfly flower (*Asclepias tuberosa*), black-eyed Susan (*Rudbeckia*), statice (*Limonium latifolium*), and showy stonecrop (*Sedum spectabile*).

Shoe box gardens. If your space is limited, you can still attract birds by using the following plants in containers: Japanese maple (*Acer palmatum*), boxwood (*Boxus*),

Let a corner of your yard grow wild and reap the rewards in the diversity of birds who will become your neighbors. Here, an indigo bunting perches on nodding thistle before attacking the seed heads to harvest a treat of thistle seeds.

cherry laurel (*Prunus laurocerasus* "otto luyken"), Chinese holly (*Ilex cornuta*), Japanese holly (*Ilex crenata*), yaupon (*Ilex vomitoria* "Nana"), juniper (*Juniperus*), mugo pine (*Pinus mugo* var. *mugo* "Compacta"), myrtle (*Myrtus communis*), and yew (*Taxus*, all species, dwarf cultivars).

A male rose-breasted grosbeak and flowering apple tree go hand-in-hand.

Radical lawn. This idea is not for everyone—or for everyone's neighborhood—but it would be a great idea to stop mowing the lawn for a few months in the spring or early summer and see what grows. You will probably see a whole variety of wildflowers—even some unusual or possibly rare ones, depending upon where you live. To reassure the neighbors that your raggedy meadow is intentional, mow a graceful path through it and make sure that the edges of the path are especially clear-cut. In late July, harvest your lawn-meadow. Rake up the hay and add it to your compost pile. If you want to spice up your meadow, you might buy potted meadow wildflowers and plant them among the grasses.

Composites such as these cultivated stiff asters (above) and wild black-eyed Susans (below) provide meadows where a variety of insects—and the birds that eat them—can thrive.

CHAPTER SIX

Get Organized

FOR OUTSIDE CHORES

The single biggest favor you can do for yourself as a backyard bird enthusiast is organize your bird-feeding paraphernalia. Having all the tools at hand makes it much easier to keep the feeders full and clean.

To start with, get yourself a bird cart, bird wagon, or if you get lots of snow, a bird sled to wheel or pull your supplies to the feeders when they need servicing. My current favorite is a long-handled, low-slung, two-wheeled cart, but a little red wagon will do just as well. Because wheels don't work well in snowdrifts, consider modifying a sled or toboggan for this purpose. It would need only the attachment of a wooden or plastic crate to save you lots of time and effort in winter when it is absolutely necessary to keep those feeders full to the brim, which sometimes means refilling them twice a day.

To enjoy the birds you've worked so hard to cultivate, keep a few simple essentials at hand: a pair of binoculars (opera glasses will do in a pinch) and bird guides to help you identify them (above). A supply of seed and a basket for tools (below) should accompany you on those trips to refill and service the backyard feeders.

BIRD-CART SUPPLIES

• Metal containers (rodent teeth bite right through plastic garbage cans as though they were ripe peaches) filled with seed. I have one container for sunflower seed, one for cracked corn, one for mixed seed, one for millet, and one for thistle. These are periodically refilled from the large, covered metal garbage cans that hold my supplies of seed.

• A large-capacity funnel that makes refilling feeders easier.

• A stiff, long-handled brush for scrubbing down the ground and platform feeders as well as the birdbaths.

• A bottle of bleach (for disinfecting the birdbaths once a month).

• Sacks of grit and ground oyster shells.

• A spool of monofilament or whatever wire you use to hang your suspended feeders.

• A pair of pliers.

• A pair of scissors.

• A screwdriver.

• A step stool if necessary to reach your feeders.

• Suet and platform feeder treats added to the cart as needed.

INSIDE ORGANIZATION

Once your feeders are restocked, you can hurry inside to enjoy the action, and unless you have a window feeder, you will need binoculars to fully appreciate and identify your birds. I keep binoculars, field guides, and a bird list and pen right next to the feeder-watching chair and enjoy keeping track of who eats what as well as when and how they eat it. I also keep a record of how often I refill each feeder and the cost and other details involved with the purchase of bird-feeding supplies. A year from now, I should have the data that will answer the following questions:

• What is the most common bird in my backyard?

• Which birds always move in small flocks? Which birds move in pairs? Which birds are loners?

• Which species are shy at feeders? Which are aggressive?

• What species make up the mixed-feeding flock associations for each season?

• What are the favorite foods of each species visiting my yard?

• How much birdseed do I use in a week? A month? A season? A year?

• How much does it cost to keep my birds well fed?

• What is the overall cost of feeding backyard birds?

• What does it cost per species?

• What does it cost per individual bird?

• How long does it take for the birds' curiosity to overcome their fear of unfamiliar objects? (With one birdbath, it took a week and a half for the first bather to arrive.)

The most frequently used tools for bird feeding: Pliers to fasten things securely.

A funnel to prevent spilling seed.

A screwdriver for quick repairs.

Bleach to disinfect your feeder from time to time.

A sturdy step ladder makes filling feeders easier.

A pair of scissors finds lots of uses.

CHAPTER SEVEN

North American Bird-Feeding Year

JANUARY

Only the hardiest feathered species—jays, chickadees, woodpeckers, juncos, cardinals, titmice, nuthatches, sparrows, and starlings—brave winter's coldest days and depend upon your backyard feeder to give them abundant high-energy food. Suet is a must in these bitter January days, and wet water will disappear down those parched little throats almost as fast as you can offer it.

Days are short and nights are long. Snowbirds gather in flocks to feast on your grain; at night, the great horned owl (*Bubo virginianus*) hoots, defining a fierce territorial boundary. Snowbirds feed in flocks; your breath steams in the air. We are deep into winter. Blue jays (*Cyanocitta cristata*) seem twice as vividly blue, and northern cardinals (*Cardinalis cardinalis*) are brilliant red against the snow. Tiny downy woodpeckers (*Picoides pubescens*) are a crisp black and white, with the caps of the males a vibrant blood red.

Evening grosbeaks (*Coccothraustes vespertinus*) are the prize winter birds. These finches descend in large, nomadic flocks, especially to feeders that offer sunflower seeds. To increase your chances of attracting them, you should plan ahead. When the maples shed their seeds in late spring and early summer, rake and dry a quantity of these, and store them until winter comes. Offer maple seeds on your platform feeder along with sunflower seeds. Garden trees that evening grosbeaks prefer include maples, spruces, firs, and box elders.

Listen to the birds before you get out of bed on a cold morning—or better yet, lie in bed, sip hot coffee, and listen to the birds. Record the dawn chorus: It shouldn't be more than call notes and twitters; most birds won't sing their territorial songs until stimulated by the longer days of spring.

It's gray squirrel mating season. Look for a line of squirrels racing through the treetops or squirrels chasing up and down tree trunks. The first squirrel in the line will probably be a female in breeding condition, followed by several avidly interested males. With a delicate turn of phrase, Hal Borland once

Evening grosbeaks travel in large, loose wintering flocks and can appear in numbers overnight to the delight of the backyard-bird feeder.

A cardinal livens the winter scene.

wrote that "young squirrels are nurtured in acorn cups." But, in your yard, if your squirrel defenses aren't up, this season's babies will be nurtured on your birdseed!

FEBRUARY

On February 2, Groundhog Day, Americans watch for the weather prophecy from woodchucks. Whatever the groundhogs decide, however, there are still six weeks of winter ahead according to the calendar. February is winter's turning point.

Great horned owls (*Bubo virginianus*) are nesting now, and their territorial calls are loud and eerie. Barred owls (*Strix varia*) start calling now, too, even though they won't be mating until March. When the snow falls, think of the big owls, warming their eggs and nestlings in the starlit treetops.

At your ground feeder, white-throated sparrows (*Zonotrichia albicollis*), song sparrows (*Melospiza melodia*), and field sparrows (*Spizella pusilla*) flutter and feed, if the house sparrows (*Passer domesticus*) haven't crowded them out of your

To some, the call of the barred owl sounds like "Who cooks for you? Who cooks for you? Who cooks for you alllll?" Owls call from dusk to dawn and can sometimes be heard on gloomy, overcast spring days.

neighborhood. Listen for the song of the white-throated sparrow: a clear, whistled "Poor Sam Peabody-Peabody-Peabody." At this season, it is often fragmented so that you may hear only "Poor Sam" or "Peabody" or only the last, repetitious phrase.

If you aren't good at identifying sparrows and instead call any little bird by that name, now is the time to get the binoculars and the bird book and learn better. Look for the white-striped head and yellow dot on the inner corner of the eye of the white-throated sparrow. A sparrow with a streaky breast with a dark central dot is a song sparrow. Male house sparrows have a gray cap, chestnut eye patch, and a distinctive black chin and bib, while females are much more drab. Male field sparrows have a bright rusty cap and a pink bill, while their look-alike cousins, chipping sparrows (*Spizella passerina*), have a similar rusty cap,

Distinctively striped white-throated sparrows breed in the far north. They are among the earliest migrants, and their calls herald the transition from winter to spring.

but a white line over the eye and a black line through it. They don't have a pink bill, either.

Look for another winter prize at your feeder among your sparrows: pine siskins (*Carduelis pinus*). They look like streaky, rather nondescript little birds, but the males have a bit of yellow on the wings and at the base of the tail. Watch for the yellow, especially when a flock of sparrows takes flight.

Watch behavior at your feeder. Which birds are aggressive and dominate the feeder, threatening other birds? Which are placid and sweet-natured, feeding in flocks and small groups?

Is there anything more energetic than a chickadee (*Parus atricapillus*) at a feeder? And what an appetite: A chickadee must eat its weight in food each winter's day. These ever-hungry fluffballs are another reason to keep your feeders full in winter, even if it means a second trip outside. Start listening to the chickadees in the early mornings. When do they stop repeating "Chickadee-dee-dee" and start singing a sweet "Phoe-be, Phoe-be"?

Nuthatches of all three species (white-breasted, red-breasted, and the minute brown-headed [*Sitta carolinensis*, *S. canadensis*, and *S. pusilla*]) spiral around tree trunks and limbs, gleaning insects from crevices in the bark. Downy and hairy woodpeckers (*Picoides pubescens* and *P. villosus*) dig juicy grubs from beneath bark. Both will visit suet feeders, so now is the time to offer your suet concoctions, crammed into pinecones, feeder sticks, and feeder logs as well as in wire cages attached to tree trunks and in suet bags suspended from tree limbs.

Male northern cardinals whistle a series of clear notes and females respond. The call is most often given as "whoit-whoit-whoit," but some of my clever students say it sounds like a video-game sound effect. When you hear it repeated again and again before being varied, you can surmise that a pair of cardinals has taken up territory in your backyard. Most folks think that only male birds sing, and while this is true of many species, both male and female cardinals sing equally well. Even more interesting, they sing duets,

White-breasted nuthatches are year-round residents in many states. They land head downward on tree trunks and spiral down and around searching for insects that hide in the crevices of the bark. All three species of nuthatches are frequent feeder visitors who are especially fond of sunflower seeds.

technically called countersinging. If a pair of cardinals visits your feeder, watch carefully to see mate feeding, when a male offers a seed or other bit of food to a female.

Osier dogwood stems are turning red; maple sap is beginning to rise; alder bushes attract early pollinating bees.

MARCH

March sees the first spring flowers: skunk cabbage, whose green-and-purple-hooded flowers smell like rotting meat. Grass begins to green up, and pussy willows wink from streamsides. Male red-winged blackbirds (*Agelaius phoeniceus*) return from their southern wintering grounds and set up territories. Buzzards return to Hinckley, Ohio, on March 15. Swallows return to San Juan Capistrano, California, on March 19.

Thaws begin, and worms appear on your sidewalk after a heavy rain. One day in March, your lawn will be alive with dozens of robins (*Turdus migratorius*) who have returned from their southern winter. Now is the time to note the changes in the dawn chorus. Robins bring the spring; things are going to get busy

Robins spend the winter in large flocks that assemble in early autumn and disperse in early spring. Flocking robins are quieter than territorial birds. They seldom sing the typical robin caroling song at this time of year; instead, their robin "flicker" call can be heard.

from here on out. Male robins have ruddier and brighter orange breasts than females, who look washed out in comparison. You'll seldom be able to lure robins to your feeder (although you might want to try with bits of stale bread), but they will love your birdbath, may take some oyster shell and grit, and will nest in your evergreen trees and feast in your pyracantha and mulberries.

Winds of spring pick up; hepaticas, violets, spring beauties, and wind flowers appear; and willows become amber blond. Plush catkins stud pussy willows. Mourning-cloak butterflies, newly emerged from winter sleep, flaunt their wide, brown wings, edged with pale yellow, dotted with tiny blue. This is our common first butterfly.

Shrill calls of spring peepers resound from roadside ponds and ditches; wood frogs cluck and chuckle in still woodland waters. Purple finches and house finches (*Carpodacus purpureus* and *C. mexicanus*) may arrive at your feeder in record numbers drawn to black-oil sunflower seed, canary seed, and thistle. They prefer to feed on platform feeders that are high off the ground. Fox and song sparrows begin singing; bluebirds become numerous and begin singing and nesting; cowbirds arrive.

Among the handsomest of birds, purple finches are seed eaters.

Mountain bluebirds are found in the western United States, and like their eastern relatives, they are threatened by competition for nesting cavities from European starlings.

The short days of spring help bring great blue herons into breeding condition. The mutual display shown here is thought to reinforce the bond between mates and help them be more successful parents.

APRIL

By the end of March, your birdhouses should be completely refurbished, cleaned, and hung, ready for the migrants to inspect and, hopefully, occupy. House wrens (*Troglodytes aedon*) appear the first week in April. You may be able to attract them to your platform feeder with suet, white-bread crumbs, or corn bread. Put up a wren house and prepare to be scolded.

Purple trillium, trailing arbutus, dutchman's breeches, and shad bush blossom in the woodlands. Clouds of dogwood blossoms drift amid leafless trees. Maples are crimson in swampy places as marsh marigold spreads a yellow carpet below.

Duck migration is in full northward swing in the early weeks of April. Herons and kingfishers usually appear in the first week. Then look for fox sparrows, purple martins, bank swallows, brown thrashers, and the earliest warblers. By the end of April, bird-watchers are glued to their binoculars as gorgeous warblers begin to fill the trees. Hummingbirds, kingbirds, vireos, wood thrushes, and veeries have flown into breeding territory. All these birds will flock to your garden if you have plenty of edge habitat as well as berries and insects for them.

Crows and small owls nest in April. Crows usually have nests and eggs by April 15; think about that while you're sending your annual love letter to the IRS.

MAY

May is the height of the spring bird migration, and each species' movements are coordinated to coincide with the appearance of the foods that they and their young will eat on their nesting grounds. The dawn

Broad-tailed hummingbirds are common west of the Rocky Mountains. They look nearly identical to eastern ruby-throated hummingbirds, but they don't sound the same. The wings of broad-tails whistle with a metallic sound, while those of ruby-throats make a mellow hum.

© Gary Meszaros/Dembinsky Photo Associates

Insectivorous black-throated green warblers will never visit your feeder and aren't common at birdbaths, but you can entice them into your yard by planting large trees such as oaks whose spring tassels (strings of flowers) will draw the insects that warblers feed upon.

branches. It may help you lure species that otherwise wouldn't approach a feeder.

It's also the time to begin sleuthing about your property to see who's nesting and where. And at the same time, begin urging your friends who have outdoor cats to trim their cat's claws and tie a bell on the relentlessly stalking hunter if they won't keep their pet inside. The annual losses of billions of songbirds to cat predation from *well-fed* domestic felines are only now beginning to be recognized as another of the incredibly shortsighted effects of our "civilization."

This is the time when many people take down their bird feeders, some because they will be going away on vacation soon, others because they think it won't be good for the birds to leave them up.

chorus is now filled with fluent, exuberant songs. Your resident birds will act as magnets for seed-eating migrants who fly by your neighborhood. Your garden plantings will do the rest of the work of attracting them and will afford you glimpses of insect-eating species who will never come to your feeders; black-throated blue warblers, blackburnian warblers, and black-and-white warblers are only three examples.

Migrants travel mainly at night, and it isn't at all unusual to wake up on a May morning and find the previously birdless branches alive with flickering, twittering hungry warblers. They will loiter in your trees and bushes through the day and then push northward again at night if the weather is fair.

Now is the time to begin offering nesting material, either from your platform feeder or tied in bunches to

Birds who are defending territory and nesting need food now more than at any other time. So keep those feeders filled! If you're going away, ask another bird enthusiast to mind the store while you're on vacation. Remember to fill your suet feeders with peanut-butter gorp, which won't melt or go rancid as the weather warms.

You can visit birds at their nests if you are very cautious and quiet in your movements. If you stay still, the birds will calm down and forget your presence after a while and go about the business of feeding those hungry chicks. If a parent becomes too alarmed and stays away from its young for more than five minutes, you must leave the area immediately, so that you don't frighten the bird into abandoning the nest.

The common yellow throat is a warbler that prefers lots of low-growing cover. Listen for its "witchety-witchety" song and look for it in raspberry thickets, in lower branches of trees and shrubs, and as pictured here, at the edges of marshes.

The intense orange color of northern orioles is always a delightful surprise. Here, a member of the western race, bullock's oriole, feeds on an insect.

Oaks are in tassel now, attracting many insects and insect-eating birds. Oaks are warbler magnets, and on a fine day, there is nothing more enjoyable than settling back into an observation post (preferably the laid-back way, by lying flat on your back with a pillow under your head) and scanning the crown of an oak or tulip tree for warblers.

Apples and lilacs are in blossom and suddenly northern orioles (*Icterus galbula*) are here, flaming in the treetops. Try to draw them to your feeder with orange slices—some say this doesn't work—or try a shot glass of orange juice. Orioles like to nest in elms and will weave their beautiful, pendulous nest creations with bakery string if you offer it. Collect many colors of bakery string, tie them in four-inch (10cm) lengths, and see what your orioles prefer. Imagine the tropical-color contrasts: a hot orange oriole peering out of a lime green nest! Improbable, but still possible.

Late April or early May is the time to put up the hummingbird feeder. Keep it up and filled with freshly brewed nectar (discard after the second day or else the birds will be feeding on alcoholic sugar water).

A female black-chinned hummingbird hovers at a columbine. While there is only one species of humming-bird in most eastern states, the western United States has fifteen species of hummingbird that will visit feeders and are especially attracted to bright-colored flowers, making hummingbird gardening an achievable goal and a rewarding hobby.

JUNE

Chimney swifts (*Chaetura pelagica*) are back in June, and if you're lucky, a flight may take up residence in your chimney, drawn again by the insects you've cultivated in your bird garden. Their "twinkling" flight will make you glad you don't use commercial pesticides in your garden.

Chokecherries bloom at roadsides, planted by the birds who love to eat those berries that make your mouth pucker. The main bird migration is over, and woods and gardens become quiet as the birds settle down to nest and raise their broods.

American goldfinches (*Carduelis tristis*) are a bright dash of black and yellow as they bob over the fields. They are the summer prize at your feeder; your reward for offering black-oil sunflower seed, thistle seed, and hulled sunflower seed, and especially for letting those thistles grow in your weed corner. Goldfinches love to bathe and will be attracted to your birdbath.

A new generation of birds begins to appear at your feeder in mid-June, brought there by your faithful clients who no doubt have told their fledglings that they know of this great little place to grab a bite.

Look for baby robins on the lawn as they watch their parents listen for worms and then gape, crouch, flutter their wings, and screech to be stuffed with the worm dangling so deliciously from their parent's bill.

Mid-June marks the beginning of flight school; all over the garden fledglings try their wings. And, as though timed perfectly to coincide with all these new young mouths that must be fed, blackberries, raspberries, black caps, and many other wild fruits ripen, ready to be harvested by the birds.

American goldfinches seem to be calling "Potato chip, potato chip" as they fly to feeders such as this thistle feeder full of Niger thistle seed. One added benefit of feeding the birds is that the calls and songs of resident birds will become familiar. When exotic migrants pass through, one is more apt to notice them because their calls and songs are different from those of winter and year-round residents.

JULY

Tree swallows (*Iridoprocne bicolor*) begin flocking on the marshes now, preparing to migrate, while the goldfinches may now be laying their first eggs. The hatching of their young is timed to coincide with the ripening of grass and thistle seeds.

Parent birds cannot resist the demands of these tiny, wide-open, begging beaks.

July is a continuation of June. Because there are so many wild foods ripening, there will be fewer birds at your feeder. But, if you are lucky, some of these will be baby bluebirds, baby cardinals, and young chickadees. You will be able to watch their first splashings in your birdbath—truly a comic delight.

Keep those hummingbird feeders filled with freshly brewed nectar and hanging in the shade.

Your summer garden should be filled with bird flowers; wild bergamot, purple coneflower, red columbine, scarlet sage, trumpet honeysuckle, petunia, phlox, lilies, trumpet creeper, tree tobacco, fuchsia, jewelweed, eucalyptus, and century plant will all attract hummingbirds.

AUGUST

Goldenrod comes into bloom this month as midsummer draws to a height. Birds have almost stopped singing altogether; the dawn chorus is mere notes and chips that only the best-trained ears can identify.

Your birdbath will be popular on August afternoons as the birds crowd the rim, each waiting a turn to duck and splash. If you are religious about cleaning and filling it each morning and if your drip bucket is

© John Mielcarek/Dembinsky Photo Associates

The immaculate white underparts of this tree swallow contrast with its green-blue cap, wings, and back. Tree swallows will nest in boxes and provide you with mosquito-removal services free of charge.

working, your yard should still be popular with birds, who have many natural foods to eat.

Northern migrants, birds who bypassed your region to settle farther north to breed in boreal forests and on tundra, begin to appear as they make their way south for the winter. Look for baybreasted and blackburnian warblers in the second week, Nashville and magnolia warblers in the third week.

Tree swallows and rough-winged swallows begin to leave for the south all this month.

SEPTEMBER

September is the month of fruits, squirrels feeding on mushrooms, beech mast, deer antlers, winter pelts on woodchucks, and bird migration. Watch for gathering flocks of redwings and other blackbirds over open fields and marshes.

If you haven't been feeding the birds all summer, now is the time to refurbish the feeder and lay in a new store of feed for the winter.

Wait for two weeks after you've seen the last hummer to take down the hummingbird feeders, because there may still be birds flying in from the north who may find your feeder. Some people worry about disrupting the natural migratory movements of hummingbirds by leaving their feeders up for two extra weeks in this way, but hummingbirds are ill designed to endure the rigors of a northern winter, and because they are a product of natural selection and evolution, they know when to fly south, and will.

OCTOBER

October is the month of color in the woods. Hickory, walnut, pecan, beechnuts, acorns, and even some chestnuts ripen, providing all seed eaters with a rich feast and nuts to stow away for winter's cold.

Swallows depart from San Juan Capistrano, California, this month, and the birds who remain are those who can feed on seeds and fruit.

Look for bird families feeding together: robins, bluebirds, chickadees, house finches.

Weeds and grasses are ripening their seeds now, giving seed eaters fuel for the winter.

© Rob Simpson

© John Mielcarek/Dembinsky Photo Associates

Northern rough-winged swallows have a distinctive brown back, throat, and breast. They nest in burrows on riverbanks or along streams, and like all swallows, they feed on flying insects.

Put up a feeder and sooner or later exuberant chickadees will visit. Listen for their "Fee-bee" call—it's a sure sign that either spring or autumn is coming. Their "chick-a-dee" song is more characteristic of summer and winter.

© Diana L. Stratton/Tom Stack and Associates

Shown here on a cliff face in Yellowstone Park, these cliff swallows are nesting on a rounded mound of mud they've built, which is characteristic of all swallows' nests. This species of swallow migrates to San Juan Capistrano each year.

Your backyard nesting birds have departed, and now is the time to take down and refurbish your bird houses. If necessary, take the time to shop for new ones or, if you're a do-it-yourselfer, order plans and make new ones. While you're at it, think about a bluebird trail. All it takes is a string of nest boxes, which you'll need to check once a week to evict any pest birds and see how the bluebirds are doing. Bluebirds prefer their nests four feet (120cm) off the ground; boxes on top of fence posts are excellent. Bluebirds need your help with nest boxes because tree cavities are at a premium in most neighborhoods. Think about it: How many of your neighbors have standing dead trees or dead tree stumps on their property? How many do you have? Moreover, many tree cavities are occupied by raucous bands of aggressive starlings (*Sturnus vulgaris*) or

A European starling is quite beautiful in its spotty winter plumage. Even though starlings are aggressive, they can be entertaining. Watch their "wind-up starling" display at a nest site, and listen to their repertoire of whistles and odd sounds.

cheeky house sparrows, which are widely considered to be pest birds. Your string of nest boxes, with openings designed to admit bluebirds and restrict starlings and house sparrows, could help bring the

Because of its small entrance, this nest box favors eastern bluebirds and discourages the starlings and house sparrows that monopolize natural cavities.

bluebird back to your neighborhood. Write the North American Bluebird Society (chapter 3, page 50) for more information.

Now is the time to put away any bird-baths that will be damaged by cold and replace them with more durable ones. It's also the time to think about how you're going to offer the birds water in cold weather.

NOVEMBER

November is a mix of winter and summer that can be as harsh or as mild as unpredictable March.

Bird migrations continue. Sea ducks go south in the first two weeks of the month, phoebes in the first week, and redwings, which have been staging for their migration by gathering in large, nervous flocks, will disappear by the third week. Many of the sparrows—fox, song, swamp, vesper, and chipping—will go south this month, and the winter visitors begin to arrive from the north, depending upon local weather conditions.

DECEMBER

Winter residents visit your feeder now, and it's especially important to keep the feeders filled after a storm, when all the natural foods will be covered with drifts.

This is the season to watch for rarities in your bird garden. Bohemian waxwings, northern shrikes, redpolls, crossbills, snow buntings, Lapland longspurs, and horned larks are all possible.

This is the season when backyard-bird feeding is at its coziest: Your feeders are filled, the water for the birds is wet, the suet is out, and the birds are settling down to feed. Shut the door on the wind that sweeps in from the north and stamp the snow off your boots. It's time to settle into your favorite chair with your binoculars and a warm drink, to put your feet up, and enjoy the birds that you've earned all year long.

© Rod Planck/Dembinsky Photo Associates

Across the northern third of the United States and southern Canada, snow buntings (above) are synonymous with winter. The males of this species of sparrow are white and black in breeding season. All that remains of this distinctive plumage when these birds fly south for the winter are large white wing patches. As you might expect, the male's wings are larger than those of the female. Common redpolls (below) thrive in open spaces and are usually seen hunting for seeds in snow-covered, weedy fields across the northern United States and Canada. The male has a red cap and breast, while only the female's cap is red.

© John Gerlach/Tom Stack and Associates

CHAPTER EIGHT

British Bird-Feeding Year

JANUARY

Chilling frosts kill many small birds, especially if they can't find a snug roost by sundown. Increase their chances of survival by providing them with roosting ledges beneath a shelter of waterproof, marine plywood.

Ravens (*Corvus corax*) are nesting now and will feed their young on remains of winter-killed sheep.

Your bird table and bird feeders should be kept full nonstop this month, because snow and ice may cover natural foods. It's also the time when birds need a steady supply of water and will eagerly visit a source that you provide.

It's the start of a new year, so begin listening to and recording the territorial calls you hear, so that by year's end, you'll have accumulated a valuable month-by-month record of who visits your yard.

FEBRUARY

On Candlemas Day, which is February 2, badgers predict the weather in Great Britain for the next six weeks. Whether their predictions are correct or not, if the weather turns springlike, robins (*Erithacus rubecula*), blackbirds (*Turdus merula*), song thrushes (*Turdus philomelos*), mistle thrushes (*Turdus viscivorus*), and hedge sparrows (*Prunella modularis*) may build nests and lay eggs, allowing the fledglings a long spring and summer to grow strong while the parents can nest a second time in the late spring and summer. Studies have demonstrated that chicks from early nests have a better chance of surviving than do chicks from second or third broods, possibly because these fall prey to nest parasitism by the cuckoo (*Cuculus canorus*). The hedge sparrow is the most common victim of the cuckoo in southern England.

When hazel catkins turn yellow, spring is on its way.

MARCH

Elm buds are swelling and rooks (*Corvus frugilegus*) gather at rookeries to rebuild last season's nests. Now is the time to visit them and watch their parliamentary squabbles over pilfered sticks.

This is the season of display and pairing as all sorts of birds from grebes to hedge sparrows begin the old, springtime dances.

The dawn chorus should be lively by now as garden birds defend their territories. Watch carefully at this time to note who's nesting in your yard and where those nests are hidden before leaves hide them from view. The timing is also right to begin providing nesting material at your bird table. If you want to try photography, consider constructing a portable hide—and March is the month to get it into position for recording details of avian courtship and family life.

The first butterfly appears, the Camberwell beauty, and it is a rare sighting.

While some resident birds are building nests, other flocks are on the move. Fieldfares (*Turdus pilaris*) arrive, stay awhile to refuel, and then move farther south. These birds will appreciate any garden berries,

Blackbirds feed mainly on garden, ornamental, and wild fruits. They also favor earthworms, insects, and slugs.

© W. S. Paton/Royal Society for the Protection of Birds.

Rooks are social birds found mainly in open farmland, parks, and downs. These colonial relatives of the crow feed on corn, berries, and roots (such as potatoes), but they also consume worms, insects, and mollusks and will feed on carrion.

APRIL

Continue to offer feeder foods this month, and if you really want to do the birds a favor, don't close your bird cafeteria as spring grades into summer. Feed all year-round, instead. Your backyard birds need extra nutrition during breeding and nesting season and will repay you by bringing their fledglings to your feast. There is little chance that by feeding birds you will be able to harm the survival traits honed by 10 million years of natural selection and evolution. Birds will naturally keep their diets nutritionally balanced and will supplement feeder foods with natural foods.

especially pyracantha and cotoneaster, and any insects, earthworms, snails, and beetles in your compost pile or in the wild corner of your garden.

In Africa, Britain's migrants are massing to return north with spring. The earliest are flocks of sand martins (*Riparia riparia*), who appear by the end of March; look for them hunting for the year's first flying insects over ponds, lakes, and reservoirs. They return to their nesting colonies when weather is mild and calm.

Watch for mistle thrushes feeding on ivy berries, which are now a ripe, dark purple. Try to encourage ivy, because it provides fruit eaters with fodder in late winter and early spring, when most other berries are gone.

By the end of March, the elder is showing leaves, and chiffchaffs (*Phylloscopus collybita*) have arrived. Look for them feeding on gnats, midges, and caterpillars in the treetops and singing from perches that are at least fifteen feet (4.5m) high. They will stay into October, and their clear, monotonous "hweet" is a sure sign that spring is coming.

By month's end, swallows (*Hirundo rustica*) are appearing singly and in pairs. In four weeks' time, most will have arrived from African wintering grounds and will return, with remarkable site tenacity, to the same nest year after year.

© Roger Wilmshurst/Dembinsky Photo Associates

Chiffchaffs are warblers with characteristic "flickety" wings and "wagging" tails that spend their winters in the Mediterranean and in Africa and nest in Britain. Their high-pitched call repeats their name: "chiff-chaff." Like other warblers, they are insectivorous and prefer the shrubby undergrowth of open woods. Males sing from perches at least fifteen feet (4.5m) off the ground.

Gray squirrels, introduced from North America, will eat songbird nestlings and eggs. There isn't much you can do about this, but you can protect at least some of your nesting birds by offering plenty of alternate squirrel food; dried ears of corn, rich nuts, even small amounts of lean meat may be offered to distract them from nestlings.

The hawthorn is coming into leaf while the cherry and flowering currant are in full bloom. Cuckoos start calling in the second or third week of April, heralding summer, and their victims, small birds such as hedge sparrows, robins, wagtails, and pipits, respond by mobbing them. Cuckoos are most often driven off, but not driven away. They quietly wait to see where nests are being made and then, when the parents are away, dispose of a victim's egg and deposit a cuckoo egg in its place. The small bird often does not recognize the interloper and will raise a cuckoo along with its own young.

In late April, cock wrens (*Troglodytes troglodytes*) are searching for nesting material and building several

When they are perched, two British cuckoos from different species are difficult to distinguish. Look for a black lower beak on a black-billed cuckoo and a lighter, yellowish lower beak on a yellow-billed cuckoo. In flight, the birds are easier to tell apart because the rufous primary feathers, which are difficult to see on some perched birds, become visible.

nests for jenny wrens to choose a favorite. The male may take the first brood to shelter in a rejected nest while the female incubates a second clutch of eggs in her chosen nest.

MAY

Gorse is in bloom, and nightingales (*Luscinia megarhynchose*) have recently arrived from Africa and are singing night and day. Trees are in full leaf now, and the easy, exciting spring bird-watching is over. The last migrants return this month to court, nest, and raise this year's babies.

Great tits (*Parus major*) have young in mid-May; their hatching correlates with the emergence of caterpillars, aphids, and scale insects. Strung, whole peanuts are a favorite of great tits, but now is the time to stop feeding these to these colorful acrobats. Substitute peanut fragments or peanut butter gorp to ensure that the parent great tits don't stuff their babies with an indigestible, oversize, deadly meal.

Seed-eating greenfinches (*Carduelis chloris*) should be appearing at feeders, fattening and preparing for the two broods that they typically raise each breeding season.

British wrens are the same species as the North American winter wren. Here, a male hunts among strawberry plants, probably searching for insects or snails to feed his brood. While you may never tempt one of these birds to your bird table, you can encourage it to nest in outbuildings, tangles of brush, or weeds.

Swifts (*Apus apus*) return to Britain in the last days of April. With luck, they may nest near you and entertain you with their screeching, sweeping flights. Incredibly, swifts seem to be able to mate and sleep on the wing. Except for those brooding young, a flock will fly out at night and circle higher and higher into the sky, where they apparently sleep aloft. Watch them funnel into the twilight sky until they finally disappear from sight. Then they catnap and glide by the sheer force of aerodynamics. At dawn, they return to their roosts, screeching as they dive toward earth.

Hawthorn, or "May tree," is in full bloom now, attracting insects and insect-hunting warblers. Horse chestnut is in full blossom by the end of May, and its five-fingered leaves are now fully expanded. Turtle doves (*Streptopelia turtur*) have arrived from tropical Africa, and you can hear their sleepy, romantic purring calls. To make sure they frequent your woodland, plant some common fumitory, chickweed, and charlock in your weed corner.

JUNE

If you have a blank expanse of brick wall, now is the time to make a trellis for ornamental deciduous and evergreen vines to climb. The trellis should hold the vines three to four inches (7.5 to 10cm) from the bricks and thus give nesting and winter roosting habitat to blackbirds, thrushes, robins, wrens, and even spotted flycatchers. Fast-growing canary creeper and climbing runner beans will grow a quick screen of vines for summer's nesting. Evergreen honeysuckle will give shivering residents a natural, snug, winter roost. Once the vines are in place, you'll also save on your heating bill.

Quiet, shy spotted flycatchers (*Musicapa striata*) build their nests now. If you attract one to your bird garden, it will return year after year and will repay your hospitality by consuming many insects.

Late-breeding migrant songbirds such as whitethroats (*Sylvia curruca*) and garden warblers (*Sylvia borin*) as well as most residents are breeding. Some residents, such as blackbirds (*Turdus merula*), are tending their second broods. There is, approximately, one pair of breeding wild birds in Britain for every human inhabitant: some 60 million pairs. Adding in this year's crop of young as well as immatures and other nonbreeding individuals, there are a total of approximately 250 million birds in Britain in the height of summer.

Dragonflies and damselflies zoom and waver over summer ponds, providing fodder for hawking flycatchers.

© Roger Wilmshurst/Royal Society for the Protection of Birds

This juvenile spotted flycatcher strikes a typical pose: upright on a bare perch, watching for insects with its large, dark eyes. This is another summer visitor that cannot be drawn to the bird table, but will nest in your garden and faithfully return year after year if you provide secure and private nesting sites, such as the ivy-covered stone walls and creeper-laden trellises it seems to prefer.

© C. H. Gomersall/Royal Society for the Protection of Birds

JULY

At the end of July, swifts (*Apus apus*) leave Britain, migrating through Spain and the western Mediterranean to arrive in West Africa in late autumn. Until December they feed at the edge of the warm-weather front north of the Gulf of Guinea on insects that are passively carried by this massive weather system. Adult cuckoos (*Cuculus canorus*) begin to leave Britain in July and early August, although immature birds delay their migration to Africa until September.

With the crossed mandibles they use to pry seeds out of cones, crossbills look like mutant parrots. Plant conifers in your yard and you may attract these interesting summer visitors.

Seed-eating finches, like green-finches (*Carduelis chloris*), begin to nest now, synchronizing the appearance of their chicks with the ripening of wild seed crops.

Most wild birds molt now, and the garden becomes quieter as many territorial songs cease and the birds disappear into the undergrowth. New plumage will replace old, offering birds better insulation against winter's cold and better flight equipment for those who migrate. Feathers are dropped in a species-specific sequence, but most birds drop only a few at a time so that they can always fly. Willow warblers (*Phylloscopus trochilus*) condense the molt into a six-week period, while resident robins (*Erithacus rubecula*), unhurried by migration timetables, have a more lengthy eight-week molt. Birds whose young look like the adults in their first autumn (for example, larks, woodpeckers, long-tailed tits, starlings, robins, and redstarts) experience a complete molt soon after leaving the nest, so now is your once-a-year chance to learn the juvenile plumages of these birds. Watching garden birds will hone your skills as a birder—those ratty intergradations between juvenile and mature plumages will become less confusing as you see them every day at your backyard feeder.

Roving bands of crossbills may arrive in June or July from the Continent. Flying in search of rich supplies of pinecones and pine seeds, they first irrupt into Scotland and then spread south throughout Britain's coniferous forests. Although crossbills are drawn to all pinecones, Britain's visitors have specially sized bills that correlate with their favorite food trees. Common crossbills (*Loxia curvirostra*), British residents who are joined by flocks arriving from Scandinavia, prefer the light cones of spruce. The Scottish crossbill (*Loxia scotica*), the only endemic British bird, prefers Scots pine, and the enormously beaky parrot crossbill (*Loxia pytyopsittacus*) is an irrupting vagrant that specializes in the robust, well-armored cones of Continental pines. Finally, the small, vagrant two-barred crossbill (*Loxia leucoptera*) prefers seeds in the small cones of larches.

AUGUST

Tiny willow warblers begin migration this month. It takes this four-and-a-quarter-inch (10.9cm) bird about thirty-six hours to fly from Britain to Portugal.

Bird gardens are at their yearly height. Now is the time to watch young birds in their first days of flight school. Baby birds have little fear of humans and will allow you to come quite close.

Swifts (*Apus apus*) leave this month for their sub-equatorial African hunting grounds.

SEPTEMBER

Change is coming. Swallows (*Hirudo rustica*) and martins gather in flocks on wires, massing for their migratory journeys.

Scandinavian migrants such as pied flycatchers (*Ficecdula hypoleuca*) and redstarts (*Phoenicurus phoenicurus*) appear this month, stopping off on their way to their West African wintering grounds. Look for them in garden trees that have fruits or berries where insects are feeding.

OCTOBER

Haws ripen on hawthorn trees, providing welcome winter forage for many wild bird species.

The first geese return from the Arctic. Listen for their calls as they fly overhead.

Bramblings (*Fringilla montifringilla*), in their winter plumage, appear from the Continent and feed on beechnuts. Chaffinches (*Fringilla coelebs*) gather in mixed flocks to gorge on beech mast along with bramblings, blue tits (*Parus caerulens*), and great tits (*Parus major*). If the beech trees have a rich crop of mast, your bird feeders may not be so heavily trafficked as in years when the beech mast is poorer.

In October and November, waves of first-year blackbirds (*Terdus merula*) that hatched in Scandinavia or Finland appear in British gardens. They will remain until late March or April, when they make the return migration to breed.

NOVEMBER

As winter comes on, watch for male mistle thrushes (*Turdus vilscivorrus*) guarding bushes or trees laden with fruit or berries. Male mistle thrushes remain on territory through the winter, and one will defend a berry-covered shrub as long as he can. If winter feeding has been plentiful, mistle thrushes nest earlier in the spring, and it follows that there will be more birds in your garden next year.

Wild crops such as acorns and beechnuts will be falling from the trees now.

Chaffinches (top left) are hedgerow residents that are widely distributed throughout Britain. These seed eaters will be sure to visit your bird table and sample nearly anything you offer. Great tits (above) are common in gardens, parks, and woodlands, where they hunt for such small invertebrates as worms, insects, and spiders. These large titmouse relatives will feed fearlessly at the bird table and appreciate anything with a bit of fat in it, from seeds and suet to cheese rinds and table scraps.

Starlings (*Sturnus vulgaris*) form flocks and the nightly aerial acrobatics that they perform at a roosting site are spectacular and well worth watching. The acrobatics advertise especially good roosting sites and attract smaller foraging flocks. Roosts are thought to aid winter survival because huddling birds stay warmer on cold nights and because information on the location of rich forage may be transmitted as the birds disperse in the morning.

Song thrushes are common garden residents that feed on earthworms and snails as well as wild and cultivated fruits and berries. Song thrushes seem to be declining in numbers because of extreme winter temperatures. Planting conifers and evergreen creepers against sun-warmed stone walls may increase the odds of your song thrushes surviving a cold snap. Dried fruits may draw them to your bird table.

DECEMBER

Some of the robins, blackbirds, and song thrushes raised in British gardens will escape southward to spend the winter in a milder climate. As weather turns colder and flocks of other thrushes arrive from the north to feed in crab apple and holly trees, a dominant, territorial male mistle thrush will eventually have to relinquish his dominance. Now is the time when berry and fruit trees are ornamented with avidly feeding thrushes. Look for blackbird, song, mistle, redwing, and fieldfare. One observer has recorded as many as one hundred individuals enjoying the fruits of a single Siberian crab tree.

Fieldfares herald the approach of autumn as large flocks appear from their European breeding grounds. They forage for wild fruits and berries in open country and along hedges found in farms, marshes, playing fields, and large gardens. Extremely cold temperatures may bring a flock to your bird table to feed on a variety of seeds, table scraps, suet, and berries.

Other berries are ripe at this time of the year: holly, hips-and-haws, and snowberries. Bryony vine has scarlet berries. Ivy berries are forming.

Redpolls (*Acanthis flammea*) and siskins (*Carduelis spinus*) who have nested and raised their young in northern Europe come south now and move in large flocks, feeding on dried seed heads and gleaning insects from bark.

Scores of black-and-white magpies (*Pica pica*), wood pigeons (*Columba palumbus*), rooks (*Corvis frugilegus*), and jackdaws (*Corvus monedula*) appear in flocks, hungry and looking for food. If your butcher can provide you with large bones and if your neighbors won't object, you might consider suspending these bones, with marrow and suet attached, from a stout limb. The skull of a cow, with skin removed so that the birds can get at the meat and suet, for example, will be a bonanza for the crow tribe as well as for all resident suet eaters, such as blue and great tits. Winter's cold will keep the meat and bones from spoiling and smelling objectionable, and the birds who discover the skull will quickly pick it clean.

In cold weather, redwings (*Turdus iliacus*) die in large numbers, even in the mildest, most southern counties of England, because snow and ice make the insects they eat inaccessible. Redwings are not common visitors to any bird table; perhaps the only thing you can do in your bird garden to aid their survival is to have a sheltered grove that will be kept relatively snow free.

Now is the time to offer suet concoctions and peanut butter gorp, smeared into pinecones, hung within string bags, plastered into holes drilled into feeding sticks and feeding logs, and hung within squirrel-proof plastic-coated wire-mesh containers.

As the massive warm-weather front north of the Gulf of Guinea moves northward, swifts that have been feeding on its insects fly east to spend the spring winging at insects in East African skies.

Magpies (top) rob other birds' nests of eggs and young, but they also feed on insects and grain. These somewhat shy members of the crow clan will visit bird tables and ground feeders and take seeds, nuts, and fruits as well as table scraps. Redwings (above) are a part of the winter influx of birds from Scandinavia, Eastern Europe, and Siberia. They feed on small invertebrates as well as fruits and berries, and when natural food sources become scarce in hard winters, they will take a wide variety of seeds, nuts, fruit, and scraps from the bird table.

CHAPTER NINE

Australian Bird-Feeding Year

JANUARY

January is midsummer in Australia, and although most birds have finished nesting months ago, rufous fantails (*Rhipidura rufifrons*), found in coastal northern and eastern wet forested regions, will continue to nest into January. Similarly, late-fruiting mistletoe may enable the mistletoebird (*Dicaeum hirundinaceum*), found wherever the parasitic plant grows, to continue to nest and feed chicks into February.

In January, the muddy flats of Botany Swamps, near Sydney, are filled with flocks of thousands of shorebirds that have migrated from the Arctic to feed during Australia's summer.

The shrubby banksias flower now, and trim New Holland honeyeaters (*Phylidonyris novaehollandiae*) as well as more than ninety other nectar-feeding species will flock to blossoming *Banksia ericifolia*, among others. If you have no banksias, you may want to try offering honey-based nectar mixtures at strategic points in your garden. Eastern spinebills (*Acanthorhynchus tenuirostris*), western spinebills (*A. superciliosus*), Macleay's honeyeaters (*Xanthotis macleayana*), and black-headed honeyeaters (*Melithreptus affinis*) are only a few of the possible species. All have restricted distributions but can be attracted to your yard if you are within their geographic ranges.

Birdbaths will also be appreciated by your backyard birds as summer continues. Offering a reliable supply of clean, fresh water will make your garden a favorite with species of grass finches. Ubiquitous zebra finches (*Poephila guttata*) as well as the more geographically restricted double-barred finches (*P. biche-novii*), masked finches (*P. personata*), black-throated finches (*P. cincta*), plum-headed finches (*Aidemosyne modesta*), and crimson finches (*Neochmia phaeton*) will all be drawn to the birdbath along with many species of Australia's parrots, parrotlets, and cockatiels. Many people close up their bird tables in the warm season, but birds need to eat and drink year-round. Offering seed as well as plentiful water will draw even more species to your backyard.

Although white-throated needletails (*Hirundapus caudacutus*) and forktailed swifts (*Apus pacificus*) breed on the coasts of China and Japan, they hawk for insects in Australian summer skies along with dollarbirds (*Eurystomus orientalis*) and dusky woodswallows (*Artamus cyanopterus*).

To the Arnhem Land aborigines living in the Kakadu region in the Northern Territory, January is the peak of "rain time."

The rufous fantail is an elegant, showy inhabitant of wet forested regions and open forests that will visit parks and gardens. It is an insect eater that may be drawn into gardens by flowering plants that attract insects.

FEBRUARY

Australia's latest nesting bird, the mistletoebird, may continue to nest into this late summer month.

In mallee (*acacia*) scrub, pairs of malleefowl (*Leipoa ocellata*) begin building nesting mounds in February. After digging a pit, they scrape dead leaves, sticks, and sand from up to a hundred yards (91.4m) around, concentrating the organic debris in the center of the mound and covering it with sand and dirt. When the mound is piled high, the male digs a depression in the top. When the rains fall, the organic matter in the saturated mound begins to ferment. The warmth from fermentation combines with heat from the sun to raise the temperature to about 92°F (33°C) by September when the first of up to eighteen eggs are laid. Malleefowl mate for life,

Malleefowl live in the dry, inland scrublands of southwestern Australia. Males of this large, wary species have a loud, booming territorial call, while females make a high-pitched crowing call.

and males usually manage the mounds and maintain temperature control by opening the mound when it gets too warm or scraping sand onto it when it gets too cool. The male opens the mound to allow the female to deposit an egg and then closes it again. Chicks hatch independently, scramble up out of their warm bed of debris, and walk away. Parents take no further notice of them.

By late summer, migrant Arctic and Nearctic shorebirds have transformed and begin to leave Australia for their distant, northern nesting grounds. Those nondescript hordes of peeps who wheeled as one in the air and raced the waves at water's edge on reed-thin legs have become more distinctive in their breeding plumage. Now, golden plovers (*Pluvialis dominica*) have black breasts and backs flecked with gold; Mongolian dotterels (*Charadrius molgolus*) become brick-red underneath; long-billed godwits (*Limosa lapponica*) look as though they've been dipped in rust. There is a continual turnover in species at shorebird gathering places as new species arrive from the south while species that have summered on the Australian coast now depart.

Brush-tailed possums breed in February. These engaging, prehensile-tailed marsupials tame easily

This golden plover is in its camouflaged plumage. Note the dark feathers down the center of its breast and the dark outline of a mask behind its eye. A male golden plover's breeding plumage contains black and gold flecks in addition to the black and white found on both sexes. The migrations of these handsome plovers are milestones in the Australian birder's year.

and will readily come to backyard feeding stations when bread and jam are placed within reach.

In dry, central Australia the most numerous bird is probably the zebra finch (*Taeniopygia castanotis*), familiar to aviculturists all over the world. These seed eaters range widely in nomadic flocks and congregate in numbers at any source of water. Installation of cattle tanks in the central deserts has allowed their numbers to increase.

Waterholes attract pigeons and parrots, too. The galah (*Kakatoe roseicapilla*) is common and the pink cockatoo (*Kakatoe leadbeateri*) is rare. In the central deserts, availability of water

Like many seabirds, wandering albatrosses become whiter as they age. While young birds are dark with a white face and pinkish bill, older birds have their dark feathers restricted to the margins of their wings.

governs wild-bird movements and nomadic flight is their main defense against drought. You can make your backyard into birdland by advertising your water supply with a drip fountain.

Migratory sea birds visit from the Antarctic. The great wandering albatross (*Diomedia exulans*), the world's largest flying bird, with a wingspan of up to ten and a half feet (30m), is known to gather at a sewer outlet near Malabar, a few miles south of Sydney. In Sydney, harbor gannets dive into the water from heights of fifty feet (15.2m) or more.

The Arnhem Land aborigines call late February to late March "close-up time," because flooding makes hunting and gathering of food difficult.

MARCH

March, April, and May are autumn months in Australia. In Arnhem Land in late March, the southeastern wind blows strongly for about a week. The wind bends and breaks grasses in the "knock 'em down time."

APRIL

Although emus (*Dromaius novaehollandiae*) lay eggs in winter, they sometimes start as early in autumn as April. Eight to twenty exotic, glossy, blackish green eggs from several females are deposited in a nest that is constructed, tended, and incubated by the male. When the yellow-and-black-striped chicks hatch, they are tended solely by the male. The mating behavior of the emu makes other national birds seem pale in comparison!

Emus are widely distributed in Australia's inland plains and tropical woodlands. They may be solitary individuals or travel in flocks that number in the hundreds.

In Arnhem Land, April's mild, dry days allow swamps to dry; hunting and gathering can resume. April to September is "cold-weather time."

MAY

As winter approaches, now is a good time to plan a nest-box trail around your yard. Cavity nesters, such as parakeets, parrotlets, rosellas, and the many species of small Australian parrots will appreciate safe and appropriately sized nest boxes. This becomes especially important as the alien, introduced European starling and English sparrow spread across Australia and compete aggressively for nesting cavities.

Lyrebirds live in wet forests and rain forests in southeasternmost Australia and in Tasmania. The long, filmy tail feathers of the male, shown here as a contracted, upright mass, fan forward over the male's back as he dances on the mound of earth he has scraped together.

JUNE

June through August are winter months over most of Australia. Although the migrant birds have departed and many resident birds have stopped nesting, backyard-bird feeding continues. Kookaburras, recognized by bird fanciers the world over, will come to your backyard handouts of bread soaked in syrup or honey. These distinctive, large kingfishers can become tame, fearless clients of your backyard bird table.

In June and July, lyrebirds (*Menura novaehollandiae* and *M. alberti*) begin to court. In Sherbrooke Forest, twenty-five miles (40.2 km) from Melbourne, male lyrebirds dance and sing on their earthen mounds. Midafternoons on cold, damp days are best for hearing and seeing the displays. Lyrebirds are among the most vocally gifted of birds, and they mimic the calls of other species while bending their tails forward over their heads. The cascading tail feathers are vibrated to show the shimmering white underfeathers that make a spectacular display in the dim, damp woods.

No bird is more Australian than a kookaburra. There are two species of this large kind of kingfisher: the laughing kookaburra (shown here) and the slightly smaller blue-winged kookaburra. Both species have distinctive calls: The laughing kookaburra says its name, repeating "kook—kook-kook-ka-ka-ka." Others often join in this maniacal chorus.

JULY

Nectar feeding is basic to ninety species of Australian birds. Near Sydney, groves of numerous tree species such as swamp mahogany and bastard mahogany flower in winter and attract nectar feeders from far and near.

AUGUST

August 1 is Wattle Day in New South Wales (wattle is the colloquial name for many species of thornless acacia trees that flower spectacularly in late winter).

In August and September, six- to seven-inch (15 to 17cm) baby koalas, the most adorable of all marsupials, are beginning to leave their mothers' pouches, where they have fed for six months. Koalas are now

Living by the ocean's edge along the extreme southern coast of Australia, little penguins are the only resident penguin species in Australia.

rare in the wild, and most of us will see them only in zoological gardens or in television commercials.

Each evening from August to December, scores of little penguins (*Eudyptula novaehollandiae*) emerge from the southern coastal waters to parade past observers and enter their burrows above the high-tide line. They lay two or three eggs between August and November. Parents of these, the world's smallest and most colorful penguins, change shifts about every five to twelve days.

The first spring songs are heard in August as yellow robins (*Eopsaltria australis*), song thrushes (*Turdus philomelos*), and yellow-tailed and striated thornbills start to build nests in August.

SEPTEMBER

The Australian spring occurs from September to November, and as the weather warms and humid northwestern winds begin to blow, the aborigines in Arnhem Land know that "warm-up time" has arrived.

The first spring migrants arrive: bush canary, white-throated warbler, rufous whistler, pallid cuckoo. Flocks of northern waders appear September 1 to spend the summer on the estuaries, beaches, and sand

The yellow-rumped thornbill is widely distributed throughout Australia, found normally in open woodlands and parks and often in gardens. It feeds on insects and small invertebrates in foliage and on the ground.

flats of Australia. These include thirty
species of waders, dotterels, plovers,
sandpipers, godwits, whimbrels,
and big sea curlew. These birds breed in
Siberia and Alaska. Botany Bay is a
favorite gathering place. Although
their numbers are spectacular, their
plumages are not. Splendid breeding
plumage has been replaced by dull
brown feathers.

In mallee scrub regions of Victoria
and New South Wales, the female
mallee fowl (*Leipoa ocellata*) begins to
deposit eggs in the fermenting mound
prepared by the male. To allow her to
do this, the male opens up the mound
and then covers the new egg with sand. The female
will continue to lay eggs through the early autumn.

At dusk from mid-September to mid-October,
platypuses begin to court. Couples swim around in
circles with the male hanging onto the tail of the
female.

Around Perth as wildflowers fill the land with
color, golden wattle, blue *Leschenaultia*, and the
bluebell (*Orthrosanthus*) spread carpets. *Epacris*
flowers are white and pink, while kangaroo paws
(*Anigozaznthos*) are red and green or black and green.
Banksias are in bloom and filled with birds.

In early spring in the western plains, yellow rosellas
(*Platycercus flaveolus*) and blue-bonnet parrots
(*Psephotus haematogaster*) investigate hollows in trees
as nesting holes. Black-and-white Australian magpies
(*Gymnorhina tibicen*) carol.

Gray thrushes, rufous whistlers, weebills,
pardalotes, wagtails, jacky winters, rainbowbirds, and
ravens congregate in gums along waterways.

September is the time when the heathland inland
from Botany Bay has a spectacular show of wildflowers. Flowering shrubs such as red bottlebrushes,
banksias, yellow pea flowers, and red-, yellow-, pink-,
gray-, or white-flowering *Grevilleas* surround bizarre
grass trees (*Xanthorrhoea*) that may be filled with
nectar-feeding lorikeets.

© Ken Stepnelll

The blue-bonnet parrot's name is a misnomer. It should really be called the blue-faced parrot. This lovely pale gray-brown parrot with yellow and crimson underparts feeds on flowers and fruits.

© Ron Dengler

Rainbow lorikeets are noisy visitors to rain forests, open forests, parks, and gardens in the eastern and southeastern coastal areas of Australia. They feed on flowers, consuming pollen, nectar, insects, and other invertebrates found in blossoms and leaves. Lorikeets travel in flocks and will also eat fruit and grain crops.

© Ken Stepnell

Honeyeaters are gregarious and colonial birds that feed in banksias and grevilleas in coastal heaths and woodlands on the southern and eastern coast.

OCTOBER

This is the height of spring, and most resident birds and the first migrants have started to nest.

In the Botany Swamps near Sydney, the reed warbler (*Acrocephalus australis*) is singing its melodious song. The little grassbird (*Megalurus gramineus*), moor hens (*Callinula tenebrossa*), black duck (*Anas superciliosa*), white-eyed duck (*Nyroca australis*), and gray teal (*Anas gibberifrons*) enliven the swamps with their cackling and muttering, while black swans (*Cygnus atratus*) and red-legged swamp hens (*Porphyrio melanotus*) court and mate.

On the heathlands around Botany Bay in spring, wildflowers are seen at their best. The aerial courtship flights of the tawny-crowned honeyeater (*Cliciphila melanops*) flash over the flowering shrubs, while their flutelike, ethereal call announces spring.

Honeyeaters are the main pollinators of eucalyptus, banksia, and various other Australian trees. They have brush-tipped tongues for sweeping up nectar and pollen from flowers.

Forest shrubs are in flower now. Waratah is particularly spectacular with its brilliant crimson five-inch (12cm) -wide flower heads, but banksias, wattles, multicolored grevilleas, pink boronias, aeriostemons, and yellow peas are also worth seeing.

On the Western plains, nomadic flocks of budgerigars (*Melopsittacus undulatus*) move to the south in the spring; they follow rains and will move northward toward the winter rains to feed opportunistically where food is most abundant.

Later, migrant birds arrive and begin to breed. These include the large dollarbirds (*Eurystomus*

© Ken Stepnell

It is difficult for non-Aussies to realize that budgerigars, popular cage birds, are actually wild in Australia. In the wild, they are yellow and green; blue, yellow, gray, and white cage birds are the result of selective breeding of captive birds.

orientalis), who have wintered in southern Asia, and the cicadabirds (*Coracina tenuirostris*). Migratory swifts from China and Japan arrive to hunt for flocks of insects. These white-throated needletails and forktailed swifts breed in northern Asia and become nomadic as weather conditions change. In Australia, they feed on nuptial swarms of beetles, ants, termites, and bees.

From October to February, male bowerbirds are building their avenues in the bush and decorating them with flowers, shells, berries, feathers, bottle caps, bits of paper, and glass. Some even paint their bowers with a mixture of saliva and plant juices or saliva and charcoal, daubing the pigment on with a stick. When the bower is finished, the male will call, flutter his wings, and display objects from his cache for the female's inspection. After mating, the female will build a nest and raise her young alone while the male continues to adjust his bower and attract other prospective mates.

From October to January, Australia's four species of birds-of-paradise are displaying in the tropical rain forests at the extreme northern tip of the Cape York Peninsula. The most spectacular of these is the magnificent riflebird (*Ptiloris magnificus*). Males of this territorial species display from a perch. Against the velvety black background of their outstretched wings, they wave their heads from side to side, showing the metallic iridescence of their blue-green and purple throats. They erect a trailing fringe of filmy breast plumes that makes them even more attractive to females with whom they will briefly mate and then lose interest in. The females will nest, brood, and feed their nestlings without help from the male.

To the aborigines of Arnhem Land, October to mid-December is "storm time."

NOVEMBER

November is late spring in Australia. Birds continue to nest and raise young and their need for supplemental food from your feeder is as great as ever.

Late spring is also the time that orchids flower in the lush jungles of the northeastern borders of New South Wales and Queensland in the McPherson Ranges. Here the spider orchid, orange blossom orchid, olive orchid, ravine orchid, and snake flower festoon the flowering flame tree and Moreton Bay chestnut.

DECEMBER

December is the start of Australia's summer. Although shorebirds will be raising their second clutches, nesting of small birds is usually over by December. The weather is starting to become hot, and in northern Australia, lagoons and billabongs are covered by the large-flowered blue water lily (*Nymphaea gigantea violacea*).

© Allan Morgan

Australian magpies are found wherever there are open fields: golf courses, large gardens, parks, ball fields. Unlike British magpies, these are not relatives of the crow. They do become tame, however, and will visit backyard feeders.

CHAPTER TEN

Squirrels: Foiling the Archenemy

"I used to like to feed the birds," my friend Connie said as we were pulling into her tree-shaded drive. "But when it ended up that all I was really feeding was squirrels, I quit!" This battle is waged every day in millions of backyards, all over the world. Think of all those squirrels. Some may be sleeping curled up in their leafy nests or snug in leaf-lined dens in old tree holes, but wherever they are and probably even while they sleep, those active, whirring little minds are consumed with one thought: how to steal your birdseed. There's no doubt about it: Once you put up a bird feeder, you have made the opening salvo in the eternal war against the squirrels.

FORMIDABLE FOE

Squirrels are worthy opponents, endowed with powers and abilities far beyond those of lesser mammals—like you and me. They are Olympic-class high jumpers and can clear four feet (1.2m) vertically—the equivalent of a six-foot (1.8m) human springing thirty-two feet (9.6m) into the air. Imagine one backyard-bird feeder watching in frustration as a squirrel raced the entire length of a deck railing at top speed and launched itself twenty feet (6m) through the air—all for the sake of a little birdseed! Squirrels can climb anything except glass. They can easily scamper up brick, aluminum siding, any vertical surface, and this is the reason you don't want to hang a feeder from your roof—or closer than

eight feet (2.4m) from any potential squirrel launchpad. And remember, virtually everything in your backyard falls into this category.

If their leaping abilities weren't enough, squirrels' teeth and cleverly designed paws allow them to seize and gnaw through almost anything. Squirrels love to gnaw, and indeed, like all rodents, they must gnaw to

Chickadee versus squirrel: Even a metal cage cannot protect suet from the gnawing of a determined and hungry squirrel.

keep their ever-growing incisor teeth in working order. If they are fed an exclusively soft diet or if an incisor is lost, depriving its mate of a matching grinding surface, the teeth will inexorably grow and curve inward, and eventually the palate and braincase will be pierced and the squirrel will die. This grisly death is a rare occurrence; most often it's your plastic squirrel baffle, plastic sunflower-seed feeder, or wooden bird feeder that

Baby squirrels are cute and easily tamed; juveniles are adorably curious and frisky. Squirrels can make interesting pets until they begin to sexually mature; then their territorial tantrums and sharp teeth can become both frightening and dangerous.

gets gnawed and destroyed. Hungry squirrels will consume plastic-coated wire; many metals will deter them, but some soft aluminum baffles succumb easily when attacked by a hungry squirrel.

GOLDEN RULES FOR SQUIRREL DETERRENCE

1. Be prepared: Baffle every feeder.
2. The bigger the baffle, the better. Raccoons and cats like bird feeders, too.
3. Know that if you hang a feeder from a tree, sooner or later a squirrel will take over.
4. Never put a bird feeder on a fence.
5. If your neighborhood is Squirrel City, use only baffled, pole-mounted feeders that are at least ten feet (3m) from any squirrel launch site.
6. Spike pole grease with cayenne pepper and give would-be raiders a fiery mouthful that may remind them to stay away.
7. Buy only Lexan or other polycarbonate plastic feeders. Squirrels will probably eventually get to these, too, but they'll protect your seed longer than other feeders.
8. Remove perches from tubular feeders. The birds don't need them, and they give squirrels an easy hold on your feeder.

This feeder presents no problem to a squirrel with average acrobatic talents—it will monopolize the feeder and frighten away the birds you are trying to attract.

SQUIRREL-PROOF FEEDERS

You may want to invest in metal squirrel-proof feeders that have ungnawable metal doors that swing down, preventing anything that weighs as much as a squirrel from raiding your feeders. My objection to these bird feeders is that they don't have the homey, friendly look of most feeders, but instead look like military bunkers. If you want or need to be this aggressive, you may want to investigate these rather expensive pole-mounted metal feeders.

There are more graceful-looking feeders that claim to be squirrel-proof. The usual design is plastic-coated metal mesh that sheathes a Lexan tubular feeder. The seed ports of these feeders are surrounded by metal and the perches are metal, too. These work because the metal around the seed ports prevents the squirrels from gnawing on the ports, enlarging them and spilling the seed onto the ground, while the metal mesh keeps paws and teeth from reaching into the seed ports. Squirrels are unbelievably clever and hardworking, though, and it's probably only a matter of time before they figure out a way to break into this feeder design. My bird-feeding guru, however, who lives in a squirrel-infested neighborhood in a small Wisconsin lakeside community, has had one up without a baffle for two years and her squirrels haven't broken in yet.

This triple tube feeder equipped with a squirrel baffle offers good protection from overhead attack. If it is hung far from any possible launch pad, it should be fairly squirrel-proof.

A cage of plastic-coated wire (above) will protect a feeder from squirrel attack, but it may trap and panic small birds who may be unable to find their way out of the holes once they have squeezed inside. Use a design like this with caution. A pole-mounted squirrel foiler (below left) should keep the rodents out of the birdseed. This feeder (below right) may be inelegant and ugly, but it is practical and beautiful to someone who's beseiged by squirrels. If the baffle is mounted so that squirrels can't stretch around it or jump on top of it, it just might work.

CHAPTER ELEVEN

Diversions for the Bird-Fostering Elite

Does the following describe your situation? Feeding wild birds has become your passion. Your garden is a year-round haven for wild creatures. As the seasons flow on and the years tick by, birds come and go, and your yearly lists burgeon. You get a reputation around town as being an expert on the subject of fostering wild birds, but after a while, it begins to pall as you get a little bored with the beginner's feeding and fostering strategies that I've described up until now. This may be just the time to spice up your hobby by trying something different, something new, something wilder and a bit more unusual.

Here, a suet log is filled and ready for customers.

THREE NATURAL FEEDERS

In winter, try to bring the birds right to your kitchen windowsill (or wherever you spend time looking out) by attaching a slab of wood with the bark left on. Let it be a little shorter than the sill, so that the rough feeder can expand in wet weather. Secure the wood to the sill with finishing nails, well sunk into the bark so that the birds won't hurt themselves as they peck at the bark. Scatter seed on this slab feeder, and when winter winds blow, birdseed will roll into the crevices of the bark, keeping it on the slab, ready for the kitchen-window birds. You should also melt some suet or warm some peanut butter gorp and press it into the crevices of the bark for little birds to glean.

If you have well-grown evergreens, consider making one into a chest-high winter cave that will provide shelter for all your feathered clients. On the most sheltered side of the tree, trim branches back to the trunk to make a cave about two feet (61cm) square. Weave copper wire back and forth to create a platform across the lower branches of the cave. The wire will support a piece of turf that you will cut from the soil. Make sure that the turf has plenty of deep grass and soil attached. All kinds of ground-feeding, litter-scratching birds will appreciate this winter cave, because it gets them into shelter up and off the frozen snow- and ice-covered ground.

Scour the woods for an attractive feeder-log to hang where it is convenient for watching. Features to look for are natural cavities, such as walnut-size woodpecker holes, and gnarled branches studded with clinging, dry cones. The more woodpecker holes, small crevices, and cones, the better, because these will be receptacles for the melted suet that you will pour into cavities and dribble onto cones. In cold weather, the suet will harden and the small-size cavities will naturally exclude jays and invite little birds. You will have created a unique and natural chickadee, nuthatch, tit, and titmouse feeder.

© Tom J. Ulrich

SKULLS IN THE TREES

This idea may seem extreme, but it makes perfect biological sense. I first encountered this unique bird-feeding method at an uncle's house, where I was startled to see three cow heads (one with long horns still attached) hanging fifteen feet (4.5m) in the air against a backdrop of pine needles. My uncle's log home had a deck along the second story, and the hanging skulls were the focal point of a high-in-the-trees bird-feeding area that I have never seen replicated anywhere.

There are, however, some caveats. This idea will work only if you have hard, cold winters, if your yard is secluded (so that the neighbors don't think you've gone mad; my Uncle Tommy lived in a rural farming community and his neighbors were a half mile [0.8km] away), and if you are not squeamish.

A skinned deer skull mounted on a tree offers lots of suet and bits of meat for small birds to feast on during the winter months. Freezing temperatures are necessary, however, to ensure the success of this bird-feeding method.

Most butchers will know how you can obtain a cow skull or other large skeletal elements with meat, gristle, and fat still attached, but hide removed. You will need to suspend these in high tree branches, perhaps fifteen feet (4.5m) off the ground, so that raccoons, foxes, dogs, and cats can't carry them off. Skulls are easiest to suspend because they have many natural holes and perforations for nerves and muscles that will be large enough to admit a quarter-inch (64mm) rope. A long, strong rope threaded through the rings of bone around the eyes of the cow and tied with nonslip knots will secure the skull. You can cleat the rope to the trunk of a tree to enable you to lower and remove the bones when the weather warms up. But all winter long, the skull will attract crowds of large and small hungry birds, and if you're a lazy birdfeeder, you won't have to keep venturing outside to refill your suet containers as the snowdrifts deepen and the winter grinds on.

SUET TIPS FOR FEATHERED ACROBATS

If you want to encourage chickadees, redpolls, tits, and siskins, take a pan of melted suet to a spruce, fir, or pine tree, and dip the tips of the needles into the warm liquid. The suet will harden, and once the small suet-loving birds realize that this resource is available, they will cling to the needles, delighting you with their seemingly effortless, upside-down gymnastics.

THE FEATHER GAME

In the spring, when swallows are building nests and flying about and hunting for nesting materials, try offering them feathers. This is especially fun for children. The idea is to find a hill that swallows swoop across. When you see a swallow coming, toss up a feather. With luck, the bird will pick it out of the air! Your luck will be best on a breezy day. A variation of this is to try to get the swallow to take the feather from your hand. Place a large feather between your thumb and index finger and hold your hand straight up over your head. Stand still in an open, breezy place, and chances are the swallow will take the feather. The birds prefer white, soft feathers but will take any color if they can't get white ones. This game is fun and is quite a reward for collecting feathers all year long.

© Tom J. Ulrich

Practicing for the feather game. Keep in mind, however, that this game will only work if you're on a hill frequented by swallows on a windy day.

This basket with nesting material is attached to a backyard feeder.

OFFER NESTING MATERIAL

Save any kind of string or thread *except* sewing thread or monofilament. These should be avoided because birds can become fatally entangled in them. For the same reason, never offer any pieces of thread or twine that are longer than four inches. You can buy commercially available nesting material or, for a fraction of the cost, save bakery string. You can also use string unraveled from burlap bags. Wash the burlap bag in cold water to make the material easier to handle, and then cut the cloth into four-inch squares. Unravel these and tie the burlap threads into bundles, which can be tied to shrubs or trees. Put out a dozen or so of these bundles in places where you can observe the birds' reactions, but be ready with replacements. The birds may keep you busy replacing the string as fast as they use it.

You can track the birds as they fly off with nesting material and spy on their nesting activities. This is one sure way to find those well-hidden nests. Watch a bird fly off with nesting material. You will probably lose sight of it, but don't give up. Walk to where you last saw the bird; stand quietly and watch. The builder will soon fly by with more material, and in this way, if you are patient, you will discover where the nest is hidden.

As an alternative way to offer nesting material, try stuffing it into an onion bag and hanging it on your feeder.

HAND TAMING: THE ULTIMATE BIRD-FEEDING SPORT

If you have lots of time and lots of patience, try to get birds to feed from your hand. Sound incredible? Well, it's difficult, but not impossible. The easiest species to hand-tame are redpolls (60 percent are said to come to the hand), chickadees (50 percent), and purple finches (30 percent). If you are ever in the section of New York's Central Park called the Ramble and hear the squeaking calls of titmice, hold out your open hand (preferably with some food in it), stand still, and get ready for a tamed bird to sit on your shoulder or land on your hand. These birds have been tamed by many New York bird lovers who hand-feed them. Once you've fed a wild bird from your open hand, you'll be hooked.

Here is the method to try for hand-taming chickadees and other members of the tit family (*Parulidae*).

1. When your feeders are established and flocks are regularly coming for a week or two, take all the seed and suet away.

2. One hour later, place a few sunflower seeds on some surface in the feeder area (a bird table or platform feeder works best here) where you can comfortably rest your arm and hand. Go inside or take a seat a distance away from the feeding area and listen for chickadees. When you hear them, go out to the feeder and get as comfortable as you can with your hand in position near the sunflower seeds on the feeder platform.

3. Be patient. Wait for the bird to come in. Do not move your hand. Keep still. If you get tired or impatient, leave the feeder area and rest inside the house.

Lots of patience will entice your feeder regulars to feed from your hand.

4. Eventually the bird will come to the feeder with your hand on it. Stay still and listen to the bird's chatter. You will probably hear angry or nervous scolding. Remain still. Allow the bird to take the few seeds from the platform.

5. When the farthest seeds have been taken, slowly move the remaining seeds closer to your hand. Your goal for the first day should be to have the bird feeding one foot (0.3m) from your hand.

6. The second day, put the few seeds at the place where the bird came closest the day before. Put some seeds in your palm and settle back to wait. When the bird comes, begin a soft conversation to calm it, but do not look directly at it. Do not swallow, because the bird may interpret this as a sign that your mouth is watering at the sight of a meal.

7. When the bird has taken the few seeds that were on the feeder, the only remaining seed will be on your hand. Again, speak softly, avoid staring at the bird, do not swallow, and before you know it, the bird will have taken the seed from your palm.

8. The bird will be nervous and skittish and will probably fly off when its toes touch human skin. No doubt it is a strange, soft texture for bird feet. If the bird flies off, keep talking softly and don't move; if it is hungry, the bird will be back and will settle more comfortably on your hand.

9. As you and your bird become better acquainted, you should wait to move your hand until a bird has fearlessly fed a minimum of a dozen times, and when that time comes, you should move your hand smoothly and slowly. A bird shows nervousness first in its stomach: Increased throbbing of the stomach means a racing heart and a terrified bird. At the instant you see a throb in the stomach, you must freeze or your bird may spook and never return.

10. Soon you will be able to make small movements and the bird will not be frightened. In time, you will even be able to walk around with the bird on your

Many species in your backyard can be tamed. Here, a chaffinch is being hand-fed.

hand. Most wonderful of all, eventually the bird will fly to you, greet you, and expect and demand to be fed when you appear. Anyone who has had a tamed bird fly in greeting will know this is a truly amazing sensation.

PROJECT FEEDERWATCH

Are songbird populations increasing or decreasing? Long-time bird feeders notice fluctuations in bird numbers and in volume of birdseed from season to season. Some years, the pine siskins and purple finches are literally dropping from the trees, while in other seasons, few are seen. In Britain, the green woodpeckers and chaffinches have similar population fluctuations. In the United States and Canada, Project FeederWatch and its British sister, the Garden Bird Feeder Survey, aim to document population changes. For four bird-feeding seasons, Project FeederWatch participants have recorded numbers of species feeding at backyard feeders. Data are analyzed by Cornell University's Lab of Ornithology or at Long Point Bird Observatory in Port Rowan, Ontario.

To join Project FeederWatch in the United States, write to Project FeederWatch, Cornell Laboratory of Ornithology, 159 Sapsucker Woods Road, Ithaca, NY 14850. To join Project FeederWatch in Canada, write to Project FeederWatch, Long Point Bird Observatory, P.O. Box 160, Port Rowan, Ontario N0E 1M0. (Please indicate if you wish to receive materials in French.)

CHAPTER TWELVE

Hummingbird Haven

Anyone who enjoys feeding wild birds at home must make a pilgrimage to Rocklands Bird Sanctuary, located outside of Montego Bay on the island of Jamaica. It is here that one finds Miss Lisa Salmon, a well-known Jamaican naturalist and ornithologist. Miss Salmon routinely gathers coveys of tourists to the sanctuary and guides them into the afternoon shade of a vine-draped veranda. As the crowd settles into rows of chairs surrounded by a potted hedge of leggy croton saplings and rioting vines, the formidable Miss Salmon seats herself to one side and asks a pair of volunteers to sit in the chairs on either side of her, which she has dubbed "the finch chair" and "the hummingbird chair." The finch volunteer is given two small handfuls of millet and strict instructions to place an open, cupped hand on either knee and wait. "Come on. Come on. Come on," Miss Salmon calls in her island-accented voice. "I only have half an ear and half an eye," says the eighty-plus bird enthusiast, "but I have a whole mouth."

The crowd laughs as she instructs the hummingbird-chair volunteer in his task: He must sit with index finger extended and be the perch for a feeding hummingbird. "I am a martyr to the bees," Miss Salmon explains. "I used to keep the bottles in these pockets," she explains, pulling at the lip of one of the capacious breast pockets of the man's shirt she wears, "but now a neighbor and his hives have made that impossible. So I have to hide the bottles till they come."

Meanwhile, three immature black-faced grassquits (*Tiaris bicolor*) are hopping on the feet of the volunteer on the finch chair. "Come on. Come on. Come on,"

Western streamertails are among the most stunning hummingbirds. A male's long tail quivers as he flies, making a spectacular display.

bawls Miss Salmon, sounding like Queen Victoria hollering for an errant dairy herd. The crowd gasps as an orange-yellow saffron finch (*Sicalis flaveola*) flies in and cocks an expectant eye up toward those firmly planted palms. A moment later, it lands on one, scattering millet everywhere, and begins to rapidly peck at the offering of food. The finch-chair volunteer watches in amazement, afraid to stir and frighten the birds. The saffron finch seems to give the grassquits courage, and soon they are feeding from the other

The streamertail is Jamaica's national bird. Colloquially called "doctor birds," they are common in the forests, parks, and gardens of the island.

hand. "You know what you're holding there?" Miss Salmon demands rhetorically. "Thirty years! Thirty years it took me to get the grassquits to come."

A pair of bright beady eyes and a whiskery, pointed nose peer out from between two potted plants, and soon a bold house mouse has joined the foraging birds who hop about the feet of the finch-chair volunteer.

"Baldy? Where's Baldy?" Miss Salmon barks at one of the small boys who serves as her eyes.

"Me na see im," the child replies in soft patois, twisting in his chair to scan the nearby trees.

The mouse is joined by a second, smaller version, and Miss Salmon notices the excitement in the crowd. "You know who's most frightened of mice?" she asks, fixing the audience with a thick-lensed stare. "Central American people. They get so excited. Ter-rif-fied. Absolutely ter-rif-fied."

There is a low, tremulous whirring, and the crowd gasps as the afternoon's first hummingbird zooms in and hovers expectantly before Miss Salmon and the volunteer in the hummingbird chair. At first, she doesn't respond. The small boy murmurs something. "Where is he now?" she asks and furtively takes a nectar bottle from beneath a scrap of toweling on the table before her. She rests it just above the volunteer's index finger and a moment later a streamertail (*Trochilus polytmus*) has alighted and is feeding. The hummingbird-chair volunteer is frozen with delight. For the audience, the ramshackle veranda, the tiers of sun-bleached crotons, the used tea bags fluttering in the doorway, the battered folding chairs, the mice who scoot across the cement like furtive windup toys, even the idiosyncratic ornithologist herself, who looks as though birds have been roosting in her pile of white hair and spattering her spectacles and shirt front—all this fades into insignificance as one of Miss Salmon's emerald-green-and-white gems zooms in to land on that extended index finger.

The bird is identified as a female "doctor bird," the colloquial name for the streamertail, Jamaica's national bird. Soon the veranda is filled with whirring wings of spectacular male doctor birds with their trailing banner tails as well as with bronzed purple-and-black Jamaican mangos (*Anthracothorax mango*). The vervain hummingbirds (*Mellisuga minima*), Jamaica's minute green-and-white species (the world's next-to-smallest bird), is too shy and frightened of the more aggressive mangos to come and feed.

Although some streamertails are too timid to approach and merely perch on the surrounding tangle of vines and call, many are so trusting that they will sit on your finger as they feed, allowing glimpses of color and behavior that only the best photographers and finest optical equipment can capture. Watch for the rapid pumping of silvery, nearly transparent hummingbird tongues as they lap the sugar water. Notice the unbelievably tiny feathers around the eye, and observe how body feathers shift color as the birds tilt in

At Rocklands Bird Sanctuary, not far from Montego Bay, Miss Lisa Salmon has introduced hordes of visitors to the delights of bird feeding and bird gardening. Her love of birds is contagious, and every visitor can have the marvelous experience of hand-feeding hummingbirds, finches, woodpeckers, doves, and pigeons.

midair. Feel the clutch of tiny claws and hear the electric vibrato of trailing streamers, as well as the insistent peep of the streamertail and the ratcheting click call of the Jamaican mango.

Other birds are attracted to the bonanza on the veranda: White-winged doves (*Zenaida asiatica*) and ground doves (*Columbina passerina*) flutter down. Eventually "Baldy," a hungry baldpate, or white-crowned pigeon (*Columba laucocephala*), appears. "He's a cheese addict," Miss Salmon chuckles, offering the huge pigeon some of his favorite treat.

Saffron finches are among the loveliest West Indian birds. Their bills are adapted to opening seeds, and at Rocklands Bird Sanctuary, Miss Salmon has hand-tamed several.

Other volunteers occupy the finch and hummingbird chairs, and everyone has a chance at the rare thrill of hand-feeding a wild creature. Through all this, Miss Salmon keeps up a constant monologue. Rather like a strict schoolmarm, she answers questions and instructs the crowd, larding natural-history anecdotes with salty observations of human frailty and modern foolishness. She dispenses recipes and bird lore as well as down-to-earth Jamaican humor, and everyone leaves Rocklands Bird Sanctuary refreshed by this unique meeting with breathtaking birds and a remarkable woman.

HOW TO GET THERE

Any taxi driver in Montego Bay will be able to take you to Rocklands Bird Sanctuary. Ask for "the hummingbird place" if they don't recognize the formal name. Negotiate the price before leaving. If you are driving (on the left!), here are the directions from Sam Sharpe Square, at the center of Montego Bay.

Take the road from Sam Sharpe Square that goes toward the sea. Bear left where this road forks. Turn left again, going toward the distant mountains; pass a high school building. Turn right at a stop sign. When the road forks, stay with the main road. Eventually you will pass a large white Desnoes and Geddes (D&G) bottling plant on the left. Keep going. Watch for the Reading Reef Club, and turn left opposite the club onto a road that leads up into the hills. Two small beer joints flank this turnoff. They are probably your last chance for liquid refreshment until you return from the sanctuary in two or three hours. Follow the road uphill for three miles (4.8km). It climbs steeply and makes several hairpin turns. You will pass Scorpio Grocery on the right. In typical Jamaican style, it is currently painted Pepto Bismol pink.

There will be a sign for Rocklands Bird Sanctuary on the right. The sign is partially hidden by tall grass and you may have to search to find it. You turn left here and prepare for an even rougher stretch of road that traverses a series of back and front yards with excited children and scattered goats and chickens.

Bear left where the road forks, and follow an inconspicuous, handmade sign for the sanctuary. The road will go down a bit, and around a curve on the right is the metal gate and cement gateposts of Rocklands Bird Sanctuary.

You will know when you've reached your destination from the screeching and twittering of flocks of finches that gather in the treetops waiting to be fed each afternoon at four o'clock. Total traveling time from Sam Sharpe Square to the sanctuary is only fifteen minutes, but it will seem much longer. Please keep in mind that small children are not admitted to the Rocklands Bird Sanctuary.

INDEX